Praise for *Sharin*

"Nancy and I share a passion for evangelization and for sharing the love of Jesus with other people. She has a really effective way of helping us share our conversion story. *Sharing Your Catholic Faith Story* is about what God is doing in our lives and the good things God has for us that he brings to others by the gift of who we are." —**Pat Gohn**, author of Among Women podcasts, *Blessed, Beautiful and Bodacious*, and *All In*.

"Nancy is a seasoned writer who has a heart for sharing the joy of the Gospel with all those around her. In everything Nancy writes, she shares a part of herself [and now] has given us a tool to help us do the same."—**Connie Rossini**, coauthor with Dan Burke of *The Contemplative Rosary with St. John Paul II and St. Teresa of Avila.*

"Sharing our faith story plants seeds of encouragement in others whose faith might be wavering. Nancy Ward demonstrates how we can share our faith stories in different situations, from an elevator speech to a blog post or magazine article."—**Margaret Rose Realy**, blogger and author of *A Garden of Visible Prayer* and *A Catholic Gardner's Spiritual Almanac.*

"If the term 'evangelization' sends you into a fit of either nerves or nausea, you'll want to know all about Nancy Ward's *Sharing Your Catholic Faith Story*. Nancy provides an enjoyable template for the challenge given to us."—**Lisa M. Hendey**, creator of Catholic Mom website and author of *The Grace of Yes*.

"For whatever reason, many Catholics find it challenging to talk about the way the Lord is working in their lives . . . It just got easier."—**Melanie Rigney**, author of *Sisterhood of Saints* and *Blessed Are You.*

"By telling her own story and teaching others how to tell theirs, Nancy Ward takes you step by step in learning how to be an effective evangelist by talking about what you know best, your own story. The world is hungry to hear your story! You just need to learn how to tell it."—**Dave Palmer**, Executive Director of KATH 910 AM (Guadalupe Radio Network-North Texas) and author of *St. Thomas Aquinas for Everyone.*

"*Sharing Your Catholic Faith Story* is the answer to 'what can I say to the next person who asks me about God that will make a difference?' In the second part of this book, I found abundant riches in the first-person stories from all walks of life, which revived my journaling routine and stirred my soul with each happy ending." —**Ivy O'Malley**, Faith Formation Director, St. Agnes Catholic Church, Naples, FL.

"As a convert who's asked on a sometimes-daily basis for the details of my conversion, I've learned that *everyone* has a conversion story, and it's good to have thought about it before you're asked to give the details of it. Nancy has put together a great tool, especially if you find this an uncomfortable topic or aren't sure how you might come off to other people."—**Sarah Reinhard**, blogger, podcaster, and author of *Word by Word.*

"We need to learn how to tell this powerful story of love between us and our Jesus. That's the first step toward leading others to a love story of their own."—**Rebecca Hamilton,** blogger at Patheos Public Catholic.

"Nancy's sharing of her journey gives me encouragement that I, too, can get through the arid deserts of life and find renewal through the Holy Spirit. Nancy's tips are the best for developing a sense of ease in sharing your own faith story."—**Virginia Lieto**, author of *Adventures of Faith, Hope and Charity.*

"The kind of personal sharing we learn to give through *Sharing Your Catholic Faith Story* brings hope to others that can't seem to let go of things concerning their past. It will draw others to want to experience a life filled with trust in the Lord in small and big areas of their lives."—**Gloria Castro**, Spiritual Companion for the ACTS retreat, Holy Spirit Catholic Church, Duncanville, TX.

"We need the right tools to help us evangelize. Nancy Ward has created a guide to evangelization that gently motivates us to persevere in prayer and listen to the encouragement of the Holy Spirit to discover and share our faith."—**Barbara Szyszkiewicz**, editor of CatholicMom.com.

Sharing Your Catholic Faith Story

NANCY H. C. WARD

Sharing Your Catholic Faith Story

TOOLS, TIPS, AND TESTIMONIES

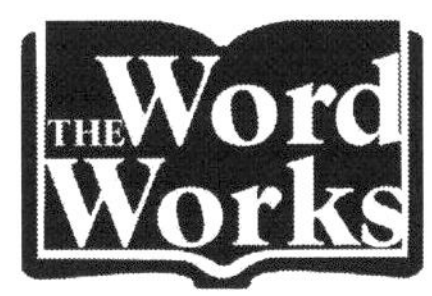

Sharing Your Catholic Faith Story: Tools, Tips, and Testimonies

Paperback: ISBN-13 978-1-7326251-0-5

Kindle E-book: ISBN-13 978-1-7326251-1-2

Editing, cover, and interior design by Lisa Nicholas, Mitey Editing.

To the Holy Spirit,
Wisdom and Grace,
Gift-Giver and Guide,
Comforter and Counselor,
Defender and Reminder,
Inspirer and Initiator of Evangelization

Contents

Foreword

But how are men to call upon him in whom they have not believed? And how are they to believe in him of whom they have never heard? And how are they to hear without a preacher?
(Romans 10:14–15)

THOSE OF US who speak with Jesus daily can sometimes take one aspect of our relationship for granted. We can easily forget that some people don't even know that it's possible to converse with Christ as a friend. Furthermore, as hard as it is to believe, many of those individuals are sitting next to us at Mass on Sunday! Even though I was baptized into the Faith as an infant, attended Catholic school for twelve years, went to Mass every week, served as an altar boy, and participated in the music ministry, I didn't know Jesus at all.

My life changed dramatically one evening in 1979 when a friend twisted my arm and dragged me (not literally, but almost!) to a Catholic charismatic prayer meeting. I was stunned by what I saw. Not only were the attendees joyful, but they were welcoming and carried Bibles. I wondered if this was really a *Catholic* prayer meeting! What impressed me the most, however, was the fact that they spoke about Jesus as if they knew him. For the first time in my life, Jesus seemed real, and I wanted to know him.

Recognizing that I needed Christ in my life, I continued to attend these meetings and felt an increased sense of peace. When I prayed, I was speaking to a real person and expected something to happen. Even though I eventually fell back to my lukewarm ways, the seeds were planted and would ultimately bear fruit. Over the years, I had many "mini-conversions" and finally gave my life to Christ in 2004.

Meeting people who shared personal stories of encountering Jesus changed my life. I recognized that he was real and that it was possible to be friends with him. To this day, I am still inspired by hearing stories of what can happen when one encounters the Lord personally.

This book contains stories of individuals who were touched by Christ and consciously decided to follow him through the Catholic Church. Some are dramatic, and some are ordinary, but we can learn something from each of them. *Sharing Your Catholic Faith Story* is a book that needed to be written. I am grateful to Nancy Ward for writing it. I'm confident that it will inspire you and give you ideas for sharing your own story. Someone is waiting to hear what you have to say. Most importantly, it's a story that only *you* can tell!

GARY ZIMAK
Catholic Speaker/Author and Radio Host
FollowingTheTruth.com

Preface

Always Be Ready

As a convert, I've always loved stories about conversion and renewing our faith. Whenever I've heard such stories, the speakers always seem to glow with holiness. The witness of their lives shines through their stories. I wanted to capture the joy I saw in their eyes.

A unique faith story hides inside each of us, waiting to surprise us as we discover it and to inspire a friend or stranger as we share it. As Catholics, we don't stand up in church and declare our witness of how Jesus saved us. Rather, we find quiet moments over coffee with a neighbor or coworker to bring up our spirituality casually. Or perhaps we may reveal a little of our relationship with the Lord in a discussion group at Bible study. We let our faith story leak out to those we trust. Like me, you may not always be ready to give a good answer.

My faith story, and yours, is our account of God's love and mercy in our lives—our personal story of "God-moments" of welcoming Jesus into our life for the first time or the millionth time.

Always, God is writing a love story on my heart, pursuing me, softly wooing me with his love and mercy. I didn't know he was nearby until I was fifteen and he swept me off my feet at a Protestant Youth Retreat. High in the mountains of New Mexico, his loving presence became as real as the gentle breeze through the towering trees. I hid his love in my heart, holding tight to that God-moment of intimacy, sharing it with no one for decades.

Through the witness of others, I relaxed my hold on my heart's treasure when I learned that all baptized Christians are anointed to be evangelists. By this time, I had married, given birth to four children, and converted to Catholicism. My few attempts to evangelize through Bible verses and what they taught me suffered from the ups and downs of inconsistency, fear of rejection, and my natural timidity as an introvert. I limited my evangelization to blog posts to anonymous readers. And all the while, the Lord pursued me through prayer and journaling, as I wrote about the heartbreaks and victories in my life that brought healing to my hesitancy.

I began collecting the testimonies of Catholics who had converted, returned to the Church, or experienced a renewal, miracle, or supernatural healing. Some simply recognized the presence of our Lord in a grace-filled moment or an answered prayer.

I also collected teachings of the Church on evangelization and learned that Pope Saint John Paul consistently taught that the most effective method of evangelization is our personal witness. The Lord was evangelizing me through the stories of the God-moments of others.

Then my website took a new direction: collecting faith stories to share, first-person accounts of the special moments of grace when my readers experienced a life-changing surprise.

But wait! I had boxes of journals of spiritual musings: inspiration I'd received from retreats, accounts of answered prayer and God-infused moments in my journey of continual conversion. But who would be interested in my story? In my heart, I heard, "Each of us is an unrepeatable expression of God's presence in the world, with a unique story." I knew I couldn't be the exception, and accepted the idea that someone needed to hear my story.

Was God calling me to evangelize with the story of my initial conversion and so many descriptions of how he manifested his presence in my life? As I prayed for guidance, I kept coming across two verses from the First Letter of Peter on the radio or a website, in a homily or a book. I kept hearing and reading: "Always be ready to give an explanation to anyone who asks you for a reason for your hope, but do it with gentleness and reverence" (1 Peter 3:15- 16, NABRE), until I knew it by heart.

What does "always be ready" mean? For me, it meant to look back on my many experiences of God's love and mercy and be ready to share them. Yes, I had felt the nudging of the Holy Spirit to share an incident in my life with someone who was going through a similar situation. How could I be ready to do this anytime and anywhere? As a writer, I needed to organize something on paper.

Keeping the "always be ready" Scripture before me as my mission, I highlighted events from my journal and formalized them into short articles. My big and little conversion experiences became clearer to me as I relived them and received new insights.

God's presence and encouragement as I rewrote these mini-stories convinced me to outline a program to help people clarify and organize their faith experiences. Then I could help them share their stories with others. But speaking in front of an audience was a game stopper. I froze. Could the love of the Lord overcome my stage fright? God would have to perform a miracle to get me in front of a live audience.

As I had experienced with the "always be ready" Scripture verse, almost everywhere I went God put me in front of someone from Toastmasters, a group method of learning and practicing public speaking. Was this the way he would heal my fear? Yes, in a year's time I gained the skills and confidence to get over my initial panic in front of a crowd—but only with his grace.

Through all this, I learned that evangelization is a calling and a ministry, much more than creating a book of my ideas and experiences. That's because we bring God's presence to others through our story—and we bring them hope in a world that is losing hope. We encourage others tremendously—and ourselves, because we are doing what we were created to do: proclaim the greatness of the Lord in our lives.

We may think we need a degree in theology to evangelize. We are all called to show God's love and encouragement as we tell of his actions in our lives and the way his love changed us. Through our story, God inspires others to discover their story of his abundant grace working in their lives.

I created the Sharing Your Catholic Faith Story Ministry to embolden people like me, and perhaps you, who want to evangelize but don't know where to start. The Holy Spirit guided me through every decision from blogging my journal entries to presenting my first evangelization workshop. On the way to the venue where the workshop would be held, Mount St. Michael School, that voice was back—the voice I've heard a few other times. The one who inspired me to write the journal entries over the years directed me to choose blog posts to share, drummed 1 Peter 3:15-16 into my head until I memorized it, and told me to seek out Toastmasters. This time, it said, "You're not going to Mount St. Michael to give a couple of talks—you're going to launch a new ministry."

So I did, surprising everyone—myself most of all!

The talks went well. During the breaks in the workshop, women begin to share their faith stories, confirming the message of the Holy Spirit. I was amazed! Some of them planned to continue sharing in their Bible study and share groups. My DVD, *Sharing Your Faith Story*, came next, and then I was ready to write the book.

We have a commission from the Holy Spirit to evangelize. He is our Guide. We now have a guidebook to give us tools, tips, and testimonies to show us how to do it. In the thirty testimonies, you will find inspiration from mothers and fathers, a religious Sister and a bishop, converts from atheism, New Age, Mormonism, and many Protestant denominations. Stories of how God used the Theology of the Body, *Humanae Vitae*, the Eucharist, Adoration, RCIA, Cursillo, Marriage Enrichment, the Charismatic Renewal, children, retreats, Catholic radio, and family tragedies to bring his presence and healing into broken lives.

Like the Catholics in these stories, I'm not a famous evangelist, but someone like you with a great story. And now I am ready to share with you what I've learned about evangelizing through my testimony. Instead of cowering in the corner, self-conscious about being accepted or rejected, I find pure joy in proclaiming God's blessings. I invite you to dive into that rarest of joys. Come join me and these blessed Catholics who share their stories from hearts of gratitude -- and never look back.

Let the adventure begin. Joy awaits!

Acknowledgments

I'M BLESSED to work with Lisa Nicholas of Mitey Editing, an unbelievable editor and graphic designer. I am deeply grateful for the support of the other members of my "team of four": my husband, Phil, Lisa, and my daughter Ivy. My deepest gratitude goes to a cadre of supporters, including my three sons, fourteen grandchildren, and many prayer warriors—you know who you are! I thank all those in the Catholic Writers Guild, especially the Non-Fiction Critique Group and the Dallas-Fort Worth Catholic Writers for sharing their experience, critiques, and advice.

Also, I am grateful to those without whom this book wouldn't have been what it is: Gary Zimak and the thirty Catholics who share their stories so authentically and generously from their hearts. Each one of these has taught me a different facet of evangelization.

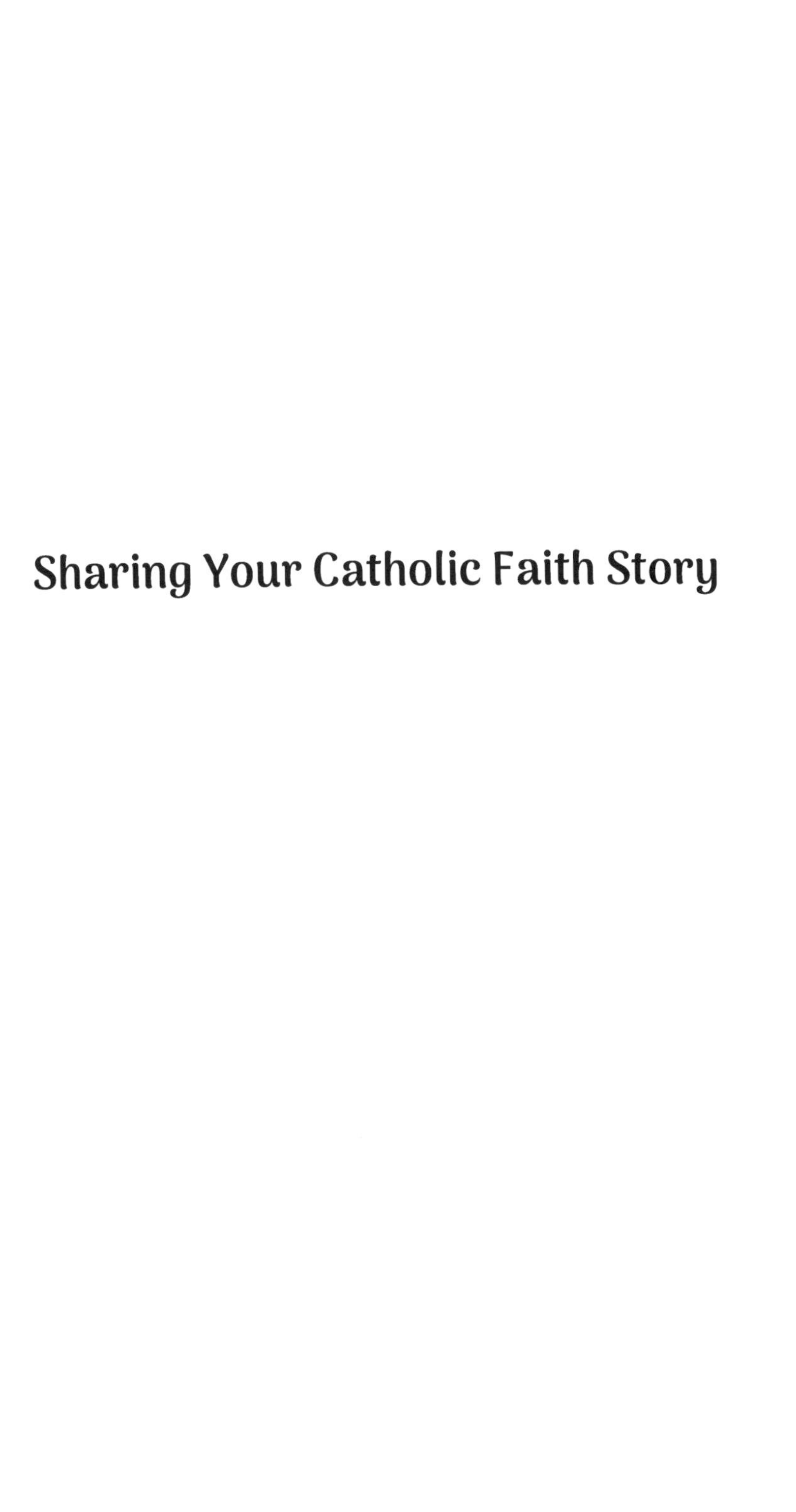

Sharing Your Catholic Faith Story

Part 1

Sharing Your Catholic Faith Story: Tools and Tips

1

What Is a Faith Story?

A RIVER RUNS through my life. It flows over pebbles and around jagged boulders. It twists and turns, disappearing into the dark underground, and then rises abruptly until it breaks forth into a glistening waterfall. This river always was a part of my life but, except for a few rare glimpses of it, I was unaware it was the faithful stream of God's presence.

Whenever I saw people bubbling over with the presence of God, I wanted that radiance, that joy! Reflecting in my spiritual journal on the witness of their lives through their stories fed my longing to attain that joy. Was God calling me to evangelize? I didn't know how to answer that call. I wasn't sure what evangelization meant or whether God calls all Christians to evangelize. Pope Saint Paul VI wrote:

> Here lies the test of truth, the touchstone of evangelization: it is unthinkable that a person should accept the Word and give himself to the kingdom without becoming

> a person who bears witness to it and proclaims it in his turn. (*Evangelii Nuntiandi,* 24)

All Christian evangelization is based on the Great Commission Jesus gives to the Apostles in Matthew 28:19–20:

> Go therefore and make disciples of all nations, baptizing them in the name of the Father, and of the Son, and of the Holy Spirit, teaching them to observe all that I have commanded you; and lo, I am with you always, to the close of the age.

I'm a writer and not a teacher, catechist, preacher, religious sister, or theologian. I searched for a way that the Great Commission applied to me. I like the United States Conference of Catholic Bishops' (USCCB's) statement that evangelization is "the proclamation of salvation in Jesus Christ and the response of a person in faith, which are both works of the Spirit of God" (USCCB, *Go and Make Disciples: A National Plan and Strategy for Catholic Evangelization in the United States,* 2002, ¶ 10). That's a declaration I can relate to and live by, knowing that both the proclamation and my response (as well as my proclamation and someone's response to it) are works of the Holy Spirit.

I asked the Holy Spirit to show me how to evangelize. How do I proclaim my faith in response to God? How do I proclaim my faith so that others will respond to him?

The Holy Spirit answered by reminding me of those times I sensed the presence of God and felt the effervescence that I detected in others. He connected those times of joy and added others, until gradually the river emerged into full view. I saw this living stream of God's presence as the source fulfilling my heart's desire to evangelize. The river of my Catholic faith story is God's ongoing work in transforming me into the person he created.

To create this river, God used people who reflect his presence as well as people who don't. He used both agonizing circumstances with unpredictable outcomes and jubilant celebrations. The Sacraments. More crises than I want to list or remember. Heartaches from losses, such as the sudden death of my father and, decades later, that of a grandson lost through miscarriage. Physical healings from illnesses and car accidents, as well as emotional healings from childhood scars and bad decisions as an adult. God came to my rescue with merciful miracles of unexpected blessings and undeserved narrow escapes. Through all these events flows the river of my story of how God has worked in my life to bring me the joy of a love relationship with him and with the Catholic Church, and how he has equipped me to glorify him as an evangelist.

While I was discovering my story, I kept recalling what Saint Teresa of Calcutta said: "Joy is the net of love by which you can catch souls." In telling my conversion story, I again saw that luminous joy, this time shining from the faces of my listeners.

I haven't always valued my conversion story. I didn't think it mattered to anyone but me. I safeguarded my close friendship with Jesus as our secret, too precious to share. My experience of committing my life to Jesus wasn't earthshaking like that of the Apostle Paul or as spectacular as the one Scott Hahn recounts in *Rome Sweet Home*. Nevertheless, God called me—shy, introverted me—to bring hope to others by sharing my story, first in my writing, then face-to-face with one person at a time.

I soon accepted that, although my conversion story is personal, it is not private. I did what Father Nathaniel Meyers once advised in a Tweet: "Show others that you are converted and others will be converted." People whose own encounters with Christ may not be considered earth-shattering or spectacular respond to how I proclaim my faith.

Yes, I changed from hiding my faith story in my journal and began posting excerpts from my journal on my website for uncountable Internet readers. I found the courage to speak in front of a roomful of people. Now I address audiences in small and large gatherings and at conferences, and I tell my story to thousands of radio listeners. The river is always my resource.

Each of us has an exclusive story that no one except God fully knows. Our experiences of conversion, renewal, and healing make up our faith story. God writes our faith story day by day, event by event, and decision by decision as we respond to that divine spark of his life that he created within us.

Here's the short version of my faith story: I grew up in a churchgoing Protestant family. I gave my life to the Lord at a youth retreat when I was fifteen, but I kept my personal relationship with Jesus a precious secret I couldn't share with anyone. Three years later, when my father died suddenly, the Lord was the only one who could comfort me—and I knew he would never fail me. I fell in love with a Catholic in college and married him in the Catholic Church. Over the next three years, I gradually discovered that I belonged in the Catholic Church. Here I could fully develop my relationship with God in the fullness of the faith.

If we met, what would you ask me about this brief synopsis of my faith story? How would you get to the heart of my conversion decision? If we sat for a while, how would I get to the heart of your story?

Whether you realize it fully or not, you—yes you!—and every baptized Christian inherit the Christ-given mission to evangelize. In *Evangelization in the Modern World (Evangelii Nuntiandi)* Pope Paul VI states, "Above all the Gospel must be proclaimed by witness. All Christians are called to this witness, and in this way they can be real evangelizers" (21).

And whether you realize it or not, you, like every baptized Christian, have a story of what God has done to transform your life. Your story is intended to reach specific people and to impart God's love to them, giving them hope. You alone are capable of reaching these particular people, because your unique story connects to theirs and because the Holy Spirit is already opening their hearts to the message they can hear only from you. Yes, someone is waiting for your story.

If you are a novice storyteller, having to explain how God works in your life may seem too vague and mysterious a project. Don't worry—first you can wade and splash near the riverbank, until you learn how to enjoy swimming.

Your Catholic Faith Story

To begin, let's examine each word of "Your Catholic Faith Story" and see how each contributes something essential to this task of personal evangelization.

"**Your**" indicates a first-person account of the facts, experiences, and relationships in your life. You make it authentic, not fiction or fantasy nor anyone else's story.

What if you were an identical twin, and the two of you were raised alike in dress, food, entertainment, and education? Suppose you both chose the same career, worked for the same company and even had a double wedding. You could write the book, *My Life as a Twin,* about your relationship with your twin and all your adventures together. But if your twin did the same, your two stories would not be identical. Each would be unique. You cannot tell anyone else's story authentically, nor can anyone tells yours.

The “**Faith**” in your story focuses not on human relationships but on your relationship with God. Your faith story is a record of God’s work in your life to fashion you into the Christian he meant for you to be, in the environment where he placed you. And yet, the essence of our relationship with God often comes clear when we examine personal experiences and relationships that have occurred in our lives, even from our earliest childhood. These are the canals and tributaries of our youth that flowed together to shape our belief in God.

“My Life as a Christian” starts with the first twenty years, when my family situation provided the environment in which I could commit my life to Jesus as a teenager, feel the tug toward ministry, and learn to rely on Jesus in times of need. I could tell you stories about my Christian grandmother and mother and never mention their faithfulness to their church, or mention my summer job at our Protestant church or my father’s death or the Catholic I fell in love with in college. But if I failed to point out how these influenced my life of faith, I would not be telling you my authentic faith story. To do that, I must dig deep into my feelings and decisions in response to what God was doing in my life. I must focus, not on what I was doing but what God was doing during those early years of my life.

The “**Catholic**” in your faith story adds another essential ingredient, creating a first-person account of the facts, experiences, and relationships in your life, centered on your intimate friendship with God the Father and Jesus Christ, through the Holy Spirit and lived out in the Catholic faith, the Catholic Church. Whether your faith started in the Catholic Church or eventually led you there, God has brought you to the Church to make you not just a Christian, but a Catholic Christian. This Divine action runs through your life like a living river that bears testimony to God's transformative activity in your life. He did not make you a Catholic by chance. If this part of your story is written only on your heart at this point, the Holy Spirit has the power to reveal it, to give you spiritual gifts to understand and express it, and to prompt you to evangelize others by declaring it.

My own "Catholic Faith Story" might begin, "The only way God could get me into the Catholic Church was for me to fall in love with a Catholic." My childhood environment and relationships are important in the backstory, but it was my love for my husband, Phil, that proved instrumental in making me a Catholic. However, as fulfilling as my love relationship with my husband is, that is not "My Catholic Faith Story." Phil will tell you that he is number two in my life, right after Jesus, who is my number one. Being a Catholic has given me vast opportunities to know God and to serve him as my story has unfolded. Since my conversion, my Catholic faith has guided my life and my story as God continues to lead me into a deeper relationship with himself and with others.

Faith stories, then, recount significant events, circumstances, or trials resolved with supernatural solutions. They include stories about:

- Conversion from a non-Catholic tradition, a non-Christian faith, or even no faith at all.
- Return to, or renewed faith within, the Catholic Church of our childhood.
- A call to a religious vocation.
- Spiritual turning points that lead us into deeper faith in God.
- Physical or emotional healings from supernatural means.
- Miracles that God works in our lives.
- Answered prayers that seemed impossible or were resolved supernaturally.

Now that we understand what "your Catholic faith story" entails, let's delve into why we share it.

2

Why Share Our Story?

In *Go and Make Disciples* (28–33), the United States Conference of Catholic Bishops gives us the wisdom of the Church in explaining six reasons we are called to evangelize:

> 28. We must evangelize because the Lord Jesus commanded us to do so. . . . (Matthew 28:18–20).
> 29. The Lord commanded us to evangelize because salvation is offered to every person in him. More than a holy figure or a prophet, Jesus is God's Word (John 1:1; 1:14), God's "very imprint" (Hebrews 1:3), the power and wisdom of God (1 Corinthians 1:24). He is our Savior. . . .
> 30. We evangelize because people must be brought to the salvation that Jesus the Lord offers in and through the Church. . . . We evangelize so that the salvation of Christ Jesus, which transforms our human lives even now, will bring as many as possible to the promised life of unending happiness in Heaven.
> 31. Jesus commanded us to evangelize, too, in order to bring enlightenment and lift people from error. The Lord Jesus, "the way and the truth and the life" (John 14:6), came to us as a teacher, opening for us the wisdom that not only leads to life eternal but also leads to a human fulfillment

> that reflects the dignity and mystery of our nature. . . . Evangelization opens us to Christ's wisdom and personal union with God and others.
>
> 32. The Lord gave us a message that is unique. All faiths are not merely different versions of the same thing. Knowing Christ Jesus and belonging to his Church are not the same as believing anything else and belonging to any other community. Pope John Paul II has pointed out, "While acknowledging that God loves all people and grants them the possibility of being saved (cf. 1 Tm 2:4), the Church believes that God has established Christ as the one mediator and that she herself has been established as the universal sacrament of salvation" (*On the Permanent Validity of the Church's Missionary Mandate*, no. 9). . . .
>
> 33. Finally, the Lord gave us yet another reason to evangelize: our love for every person, whatever his or her situation, language, physical, mental, or social condition. Because we have experienced the love of Christ, we want to share it. . . .

In love, Jesus commanded us to evangelize to bring others to the salvation he offers everyone, to enlighten those in error, and bring them in union with God in Heaven. The Lord's message is unique and two-fold: God loves all people and wants them to be saved, and God has established Christ and the Church as the "universal sacrament of salvation." We know Christ's love and want to share it freely with everyone without discrimination.

In faith and love, we keep these solid truths in mind as the bedrock for sharing our story, as we discover in detail many ways to evangelize through our witness in everyday situations.

Benefits of Sharing Your Story

Evangelization is part and parcel of being a Christian, but sharing our faith is not simply a chore to be carried out. When we share our faith stories with others, not only do we grow as Christians, but we encourage others and give glory to God.

Growing as Christians

When we share our faith stories, we fully live our baptismal commission. During the baptismal rite (1970), one of the intercessions offered on behalf of the newly baptized is: "Through baptism and confirmation, make him (her) your faithful follower and a witness to your Gospel." So, from the moment of our baptism, along with our new life in Christ we also receive this call to offer that life to God for others by witnessing to the Gospel. We also were equipped to evangelize through the intercessions to "free him (her) from original sin, make him (her) a temple of your glory and send your Holy Spirit to dwell with him (her)."

I was first baptized as a Protestant and later conditionally baptized as a Catholic (as was the custom before Vatican II). For me, the effects of baptism have been a tremendous source of joy. That's when I was adopted as a beloved daughter of God, equipped as a follower, commissioned to witness, freed from original sin, made a temple of his glory, empowered by the Holy Spirit, welcomed into the Church, and lovingly placed into the river of my faith story.

My baptism gave me my identity in Christ and began God's work in my life. May I never "dry out" and turn away from being his beloved daughter, whom he continues to transform.

We examine our life and reconcile with God and others. As I recall my story, I've received the grace to evaluate my life. Exploring different quandaries in it—those boulders that block the flow to a trickle—prompts me to make amends, to forgive and ask forgiveness, including celebrating the Sacrament of Reconciliation. I have become comfortable asking the Holy Spirit for wisdom about things I don't understand and trusting God when answers do not come. Primarily, self-examination leads me to gratefulness to God for his merciful and loving care.

We experience God's power in us. In John 10:10, Jesus says that he has come that we may have abundant life. This life of abundance comes as we open ourselves to receive power in the gifts of the Holy Spirit and enjoy the fruits of the Holy Spirit. His power works within us for his glory, as we see in the prayer of Ephesians 3:20–21:

> Now to him who is able to accomplish far more than all we ask or imagine, by the power at work within us, to him be glory in the Church and in Christ Jesus to all generations, forever and ever. Amen.

God's power comes to us through the gifts of the Holy Spirit, which the *Catechism of the Catholic Church* (CCC) identifies as wisdom, understanding, counsel, fortitude, knowledge, piety, and fear of the Lord (CCC 1845).

Living our Christian life with these powerful gifts produces the fruits of the Spirit, which are the evidence of the abundant life Jesus promised. The Catechism teaches us that:

> The fruits of the Spirit are perfections that the Holy Spirit forms in us as the first fruits of eternal glory. The tradition of the Church lists twelve of them "charity, joy, peace, patience, kindness, goodness, generosity, gentleness, faithfulness, modesty, self-control, chastity." (1 Cor 12 in CCC 1832)

We share in the Great Commission. We share the honor of our calling as evangelists with the first Apostles. Evangelization is the major purpose of the Great Commission (Matthew 28: 16–28) that Jesus gave his followers, to spread the faith into the whole world. In our little circle of influence, sharing our story is essential in becoming God's co-workers as evangelists—and also in strengthening our faith. Evangelization is a ministry of giving back to God, who is generosity itself. Like any act of Christian charity, sharing our story brings us the reward of knowing we gave of ourselves to provide what others need without expecting payback. Because sharing our story brings others closer to Christ, the warm feelings of accomplishing something for God are worth any sacrifice we bear.

The personal benefits of evangelizing go way beyond warm feelings, however, which may not always come. God never fails to reward obedience to his will and to bless us abundantly. As 2 Corinthians 9:8 assures us, "God is able to provide you with every blessing in abundance, so that you may always have enough of everything and may provide in abundance for every good work." When we share our story, our faith grows exponentially, no matter how those listening react at the moment. We can never be as generous to others as God is to us, but we can give to others a little of the faith we have received from those God has used to mentor us.

We embrace our God-given identity. When I contemplate my identity as a beloved daughter of God, I am moved by how deeply he loves me.

He pursues a close relationship with all of us, the way we might pursue a wayward child. God does everything in his power to win us back without forcing us against our will. We cannot imagine to what extremes he goes to fight for our souls. Once we allow his never-ending love to overwhelm us, we have the confident assurance found in the saints that he is always with us. When we share our story, we rely on him to overshadow us and to carry us through with his grace, and to speak his message of hope through us. Sharing our Catholic faith story is how we live out our God-given identity as Spirit-filled evangelists, as St. Paul assures us in his Letter to the Philippians: "I am sure that he who began a good work in you will bring it to completion at the day of Jesus Christ" (Philippians 1:6).

We express our love for God. We can gather up all the rewards for evangelizing and they mean nothing unless we are doing it all for God. Evangelizing is our purest way to declare our love and thankfulness for all that God is to us, much less all he has given us. We are only cooperating as he completes the work he began.

We need to evangelize! Beyond any other benefits, it allows us to pour out our love for God and to God, and to acknowledge his love for us. Evangelizing is all about love.

Evangelization fulfills the command to love God by acknowledging to ourselves and others how he has always saved, forgiven, guided, and supported us. As Jesus commands us in Mark 12:30, "You shall love the Lord your God with all your heart, and with all your soul, and with all your mind, and with all your strength." When we willingly share our unique story with someone whom the Holy Spirit has prepared to hear it at that unrepeatable moment, we are loving God in a one-of-a-kind way. No matter what happens, we are fulfilling our commitment to follow where his Spirit leads and to minister right here, right now. We pour out our heartfelt love for him in our story to others as perfume on his feet. In these moments, no one else is there to love him like we can with joyful abandon.

Encouraging others

When we share our story, we nourish and encourage those who hear it. God uses our story to nourish others with his loving presence. People around us are attracted to the slightest hint of the Lord in our testimony amid our myriad of weaknesses. Why? Because they can relate to our imperfections as well as our humility. God's infinite power and glory contrasts with their great need and lavishly fills it.

And what an audience we have! Good people everywhere are striving for peace and longing for hope—both online and offline. The Pew 2014 US Religious Landscape Survey, showed that 15% of Catholics shared their faith online and 39% saw others do so. And, offline, 38% of Catholics shared their faith in person. We can be the inspired consumers and motivated providers of faith stories both online and off. Wherever we interact with others, our involvement in evangelization brings God's presence to them.

Think of one person in the pew or a Facebook friend who doesn't know God loves him or her personally. Imagine what it would mean to that person if you could bring God's love into that one life!

We engage in spiritual works of mercy. When we share our faith story, we aren't showing off, we are helping others in their spiritual need. The *Catechism* defines "works of mercy" as:

> charitable actions by which we come to the aid of our neighbor in his spiritual and bodily necessities. Instructing, advising, consoling, comforting are spiritual works of mercy, as are forgiving and bearing wrongs patiently. (CCC 2447)

Here are three examples of how our story can be helpful in our works of mercy:

- We can "counsel the doubtful" by demonstrating our faith through the witness of our life so that others may see God's love revealed through our words and actions.
- We can "instruct the ignorant" as we talk about how God loves us, forgives us, heals us, and transforms us. We do that best by sharing stories of our struggles and God's faithfulness.
- We can "comfort the afflicted" by listening and comforting those who are dealing with grief. When we can't find the words to console them, the Holy Spirit will prompt us with an incident in our story when God was faithful during our loss.

We reflect and connect Jesus to others. Our story makes Jesus real to those whom the Holy Spirit prepares to receive it. We are reflections of Christ to others. God expresses his love through our stories. The life of Jesus living in us connects with his life living in others, activates their faith, and strengthens our faith as we share our stories. They get to know Jesus Christ through our stories.

We give glory to God

We are not evangelizing for our own glory, but to glorify God. Sharing our story is not about showing how pious or holy we have become, but how God's love for us has transformed us. We acknowledge his power and might in showing how he has been able to bring good even out of our neglect and sin.

For our good, God commands us to glorify him, for it is only by living to glorify him that we can be truly holy and happy, as St. Paul wrote in Philippians 4:12–13:

> I know indeed how to live in humble circumstances; I also know how to live with abundance. In every circumstance and in all things I have learned the secret of being well fed and of going hungry, of living in abundance and of being in need. I have the strength for everything through him who empowers me.

Therefore, we share our story for the glory of God to work through Christ within us for the benefit of others.

We share in God's divine life as he created us to do. He willed this purpose for us to enjoy abundant life. When we share our story, his glory shines forth through his divine life within us. Others see him glorified in our story and they, in turn, glorify him. Saint Matthew put it this way: "Let your light so shine before men, that they may see your good works and give glory to your Father who is in heaven." (Matthew 5:16).

We build God's kingdom. The parable of the workers in the vineyard in Matthew 20 describes God's attitude toward those who work to build the kingdom and those who won't. As God's co-workers, we build his kingdom not only in formal ministries as teachers, religious education instructors, pro-life advocates, but also as nurturing parents, faithful spouses, honest employees, and helpful neighbors. The Holy Spirit prompts us where and when to evangelize. Our calling to evangelize encompasses every facet of our lives, including those we know and those silent observers of our faith walk who have yet to ask us about our story.

We uphold God's reputation. We represent him by proclaiming the wonders he has done in our lives. Remember that we speak for our Lord Jesus Christ. Our confidence is in his power to speak through us. He is the way, the truth, and the life—that's the connection that we can reinforce in ourselves—and the connection we help others strengthen as we share how he transforms our lives. I love how Saint Peter sums it up:

> Sanctify Christ as Lord in your hearts. Always be ready to give an explanation to anyone who asks you for a reason for your hope, but do it with gentleness and reverence. (1 Peter 3:15–16, NABRE)

All God needs to water the arid hearts of those we meet is our smile, a listening ear, or a spontaneous word of encouragement as we relate an incident of God's grace that changed us. We can bring little drops of God's grace into the lives of a new acquaintance or a long-troubled relationship. Like the morning dew, our witness can be a trickle of the Lord's living water to soften the hard ground of the hearts of those not yet ready for a watershed of evangelization.

Ask Yourself: Am I surprised by any of the ways that sharing our faith story benefits ourselves and others and gives glory to God? Which one struck the deepest chord in my heart?

3

Faith Brings Us to Witness Like Mary

GOD CHOSE MARY as the first evangelist. She said "yes" because she trusted him. She embraced his mission for her life and brought the presence of Jesus to the world through the power of the Holy Spirit. As our model for becoming evangelists, Mary demonstrates the character traits we need: humility, obedience, authentic witness, joyful praise, and close relationship with God the Father, Jesus Christ, and the Holy Spirit. Everything she did was a testimony of God's love.

Mary epitomizes faith in God. She exemplifies the motivation for becoming an evangelist by demonstrating what faith is. Pope Francis may have had Mary in mind when he said, "Faith is an encounter with Jesus Christ, with God, from which faith is born, and from there it brings you to witness" (Homily, Feb. 21, 2014).

Encounter with the Lord

The Virgin Mary experienced just such an encounter at the Annunciation. Her unwavering faith brought her a visit from God's messenger and empowered her to fulfill her life's mission to bring Jesus, our Savior, to us, as St. Luke tells us:

> In the sixth month the angel Gabriel was sent from God to a city of Galilee named Nazareth, to a virgin betrothed to a man whose name was Joseph, of the house of David; and the virgin's name was Mary. And he came to her and said, "Hail, full of grace, the Lord is with you!" But she was greatly troubled at the saying, and considered in her mind what sort of greeting this might be. (Luke 1:26–29)

Mary trusted God so completely that, even though Gabriel's mysterious salutation alarmed her, she didn't hesitate to ask him what his greeting meant. Mary's unfailing faith inspires me to strive to know and love God so much that I trust him in sudden encounters as she did. When I face an unexpected sharp turn, can I question his messenger with the confidence of his beloved child?

Even more puzzling to Mary than the strange greeting was the news that she would give birth to the Messiah! Gabriel informs her of God's mission for her alone, which is possible only through God.

> And the angel said to her, "Do not be afraid, Mary, for you have found favor with God. And behold, you will conceive in your womb and bear a son, and you shall call his name Jesus. He will be great, and will be called the Son of the Most High; and the Lord God will give to him the throne

> of his father David, and he will reign over the house of Jacob for ever; and of his kingdom there will be no end." And Mary said to the angel, "How shall this be, since I have no husband?" (Luke 1:30–34)

Did you know that God has a unique mission for each of us that is possible only through him?

Her dialogue with Gabriel empowered Mary to ask questions with expectant faith. With the perseverance of Abraham, she asked for more information to clarify how she could fulfill this impossible mission for God. We, too, can seek clarification in life's pivotal moments by questioning God during our prayer time at home, or (even better) before the Blessed Sacrament, and listening to the guidance of the Holy Spirit.

The angel explained to Mary how God would miraculously make the impossible a reality to bring about his will for her life:

> And the angel said to her, "The Holy Spirit will come upon you, and the power of the Most High will overshadow you; therefore the child to be born will be called holy, the Son of God." (Luke 1:35)

Do we see examples around us of God's power overshadowing someone and overriding logic and human efforts? Miracle stories of unheard-of healings and unbelievable sacrifices? A Polish priest, St. Maximillian Kolbe, gave his life for a family man in a German concentration camp; an expectant mother, St. Gianna Molla, died of cancer rather than abort her baby girl.

Before Mary could ask another question, the angel revealed Elizabeth's pregnancy, an example of how the power of God makes all things possible to fulfill his will.

> And behold, your kinswoman Elizabeth in her old age has also conceived a son; and this is the sixth month with her who was called barren. For with God nothing will be impossible. (Luke 1:36–37)

What a shock to Mary! Yes, even though God had prepared her for this most exalted role in his kingdom, she must have been stunned. Did Gabriel's sudden appearance and incredible mission for her seem unreal to her?

The news of Elizabeth's pregnancy at her advanced age gave Mary the fervent desire to go and help her cousin. As no one else would, Elizabeth would understand what was happening to Mary. The two expectant mothers, one old and nearing the end of her miraculous pregnancy, one young and at the beginning of hers, needed each other.

Surely the Holy Spirit guided Mary in her *fiat* of surrender to God's will as she became his spouse.

> And Mary said, "Behold, I am the handmaid of the Lord; let it be done to me according to your word." And the angel departed from her. (Luke 1:38)

Mary said "yes," and even though she didn't know everything she wanted to know, she trusted God.

Her "yes" triggered a new level of God's power in her through the Holy Spirit. She was completely open to his guidance in following God's will. We have the Holy

Spirit guiding us in every "yes" of surrender to God's will. The more we open ourselves to the Holy Spirit, the more power he gives us to follow God's plan for us.

Moved to Witness

Mary's powerful encounter with Gabriel compelled her to witness. The Holy Spirit overwhelmed her with such joy that she could only respond by telling those dearest to her what God had done in her—as the angel had directed her.

> In those days Mary arose and went with haste into the hill country, to a city of Judah and she entered the house of Zechariah and greeted Elizabeth. (Luke 1:39–40)

She immediately traveled to visit her cousin Elizabeth. The distance of about eighty miles, taking four or five days travel, gave Mary the opportunity she needed to ponder the meaning of what God was doing through her. Gabriel returned to Heaven but the Holy Spirit walked beside Mary, guiding her way, reassuring her, answering as many of her questions as she could handle, and clarifying her mission.

What questions did Mary ponder on her way to visit Elizabeth? What answers did she get?

When I am traveling only a few hours on an airplane, I often will use that time to ask God questions in my journal about bewildering unknowns in my life. Like Mary, I may ask: Why do you bless me abundantly and then send me on a hard journey? How do you want me to handle my current circumstance? What do I do next?

What hardships lie ahead? How is this mission you have given me going to work out? How do I handle the scoffers who criticize my faithfulness to you? With whom can I share my joy in the Lord freely? Or bring new life in the Holy Spirit to those I meet?

I don't know how many answers Mary received. In her openness to the Holy Spirit, she probably received many more answers than I do. Sometimes, I understand some of the unknowns better by the time I arrive at my destination. Sometimes, I must accept the unknowns as gifts to open another day.

Mary greeted Elizabeth and, before she could give her cousin the news of her own miraculous pregnancy, God announced it when the baby, John the Baptist, leaped in Elizabeth's womb, again proving that nothing is impossible with God. In the presence of Mary with Jesus in her womb, the Holy Spirit filled Elizabeth with the Holy Spirit.

> And when Elizabeth heard the greeting of Mary, the babe leaped in her womb; and Elizabeth was filled with the Holy Spirit and she exclaimed with a loud cry, "Blessed are you among women, and blessed is the fruit of your womb! And why is this granted me, that the mother of my Lord should come to me? For behold, when the voice of your greeting came to my ears, the babe in my womb leaped for joy. And blessed is she who believed that there would be a fulfillment of what was spoken to her from the Lord." (Luke 1:41–45)

Having pondered her story on her journey, Mary was ready to share it. The Holy Spirit prepared Elizabeth to receive the Good News when John leaped in her womb in the presence of Jesus, her Lord. As Mary gave the details of Gabriel's announcement, the overshadowing of the Holy Spirit, and her pregnancy, the angel's visitation became more vivid, more powerful, and more real. Each time she relived the Annunciation scene, Mary grew surer of her mission.

When you mull over an incredible event in your life, does the reality slowly sink in over time? Can you see the advantages and disadvantages it could bring? An unexpected pregnancy can bring joy or frustration. Your reactions may range from delight to disappointment, from wanting to shout from the mountaintop to fleeing into hiding. Finally, you come to accept God's will, even if the outcome is the opposite of what you thought was best for you. It's human—and healthy—to question and ponder puzzling changes until you are blessed with the peace that God meant you to have in the center of his will.

Mary's questioning of the angel during the Annunciation, as well as her pondering during her journey, made the action of the Holy Spirit clearer in her mind when she shared it.

During the time Mary stayed with her cousin, imagine what questions Elizabeth must have asked! In the same way, the reactions and questions of Elizabeth, whom the Holy Spirit had prepared to receive Mary's story, made her encounter more powerful and real. When we tell our faith story that ends in God's glory, we witness authentically. Others see the backstory of how we made the decision to follow God's will and why we do it with so much joy.

Our "Magnificat"

We, too, can trust God and say "yes" to our calling as evangelists. Our authentic witness begins with our openness to the Holy Spirit. That vulnerability leads to a holy encounter that changes us so that our witness flows from our relationship with Jesus. Knowing and pondering our story clarifies it and fills us with joy that overflows to others. We can bring the presence of Jesus within us into the world with humility and joy, through the gifts and power of the Holy Spirit.

Like Mary, when we share our story, we see how God intervened and steered us to the path he planned for our greatest happiness. Then our deepest beliefs naturally emerge in joyful praise—like Mary's Magnificat:

> "My soul magnifies the Lord, and my spirit rejoices in God my Savior . . . for he who is mighty has done great things for me, and holy is his name." (Luke 1:46–47, 49)

With faith surging from an unshakable trust in God, Mary encountered God, who transformed her into the Mother of God and the first evangelist, the first to share the presence of Jesus within her. Our trickle of faith can lead us to a God-moment and begin our transformation into an evangelist sparkling with that joy of Emmanuel, God our Savior with us, as Mary did. In her, we find the example of persistent faith to trust God, the courage to ask him questions, and the grace to commit our lives to him. He narrates our story to draw us closer to him and prepare us to share with those he brings into the course of our lives.

Mary was an extraordinary evangelist, filled with the Holy Spirit. We are called as everyday evangelists with the grace of the Holy Spirit, as she was. Bishop Emeritus Sam Jacobs of Houma-Thibodaux, LA, in *John Paul II and the New Evangelization*, quotes Pope St. John Paul as saying:

> "It is the grace of the Spirit that triggers the response of faith and deeper commitment in the person who freely chooses to say yes to Jesus' call and plan. The evangelist is merely a chosen instrument in the hands of God, though an important one." (44)

Ask Yourself: What response of deeper commitment is the grace of the Holy Spirit triggering in me? What unique faith story hides in my heart, waiting to fill me with joy?

4

Start with Your Spiritual Journal

IF WE ARE MEANT to be evangelists, as unique expressions of God's presence, how do we start?

Saint John Paul II coined the term "the new evangelization." In reiterating this call in his message to World Youth Day attendees in 2005, he said:

> The Church needs genuine witnesses for the new evangelization: men and women whose lives have been transformed by meeting with Jesus, men and women who are capable of communicating this experience to others. (7)

We fulfill our baptismal call to evangelize, with the new fervor of the new evangelization, by sharing an experience of conversion, renewal, or healing from our faith story every time God gives us an opportunity.

One of the fundamental tools of evangelization emphasized in the early Church as well as the new evangelization is our firsthand witness of how we met the Lord Jesus, and what he is doing in our lives. Witnessing requires that we stop being content to know *about* the Lord, and get to know the Lord himself, personally and intimately. We want to witness from our hearts, not our heads. Regardless of our hesitancy to put into words our personal relationship with the Lord, much less share it aloud, we cannot hand on what we profess to believe unless it matches what we do privately and publicly.

The Apostles knew how to tell the story of how they met the Lord and developed a relationship with him, and how he transformed their hearts and therefore their lives. The events in the life of Jesus, from his first miracle at Cana through his passion, death, resurrection, and ascension, lived in their hearts. Their testimony-based evangelization came from what they had seen and heard from the Lord, not something they quoted from the story of someone else.

We have to be able to tell our story of how we met the Lord, and how our relationship with him is changing our lives. Like all evangelists, new or old, we are called to speak the truth of the faith as revealed in our experience and relationship with Jesus Christ—yes, that scary, vulnerable, stepping out in faith to share what God has done in our lives and how he transformed our hearts.

As "genuine witnesses for the new evangelization (. . .) whose lives have been transformed by meeting with Jesus," we can wing it—or we can be ready and effective, as those "who are capable of communicating this experience to others."

This book promises tools, tips, and testimonies. Journaling is the first of five tools that take us from wishful thinking to proactive evangelization. Our spiritual journal is crucial in preparing to share our faith stories effectively.

In the first chapter, I mentioned that I had at first "hidden" my faith story in my spiritual journal and later began sharing my story by posting excerpts from that journal on my website. So, just what do I mean by a "spiritual journal"?

A Journal Versus a Spiritual Journal

A journal of any kind is a way of writing about your life, as opposed to other things you might write: vacation dreams, career plans, business strategies, bucket lists, or health and fitness goals. Scientific research finds that journaling can enhance your life in remarkable ways that benefit your mind, emotions, relationships, confidence, creativity, communication, and self-discipline. A journal is written by you for your own benefit.

When you call on the power of the Holy Spirit, however, you add a spiritual dimension to your journaling. The results bring so much more than self-improvements or an enhanced lifestyle. All of the advantages of journaling can be yours, but the Holy Spirit can add a mystical dimension to them that unifies your spirit with the Holy Spirit.

A spiritual journal is by you, yet inspired by the Holy Spirit. It is usually addressed to God, to grow your relationship with him. You might address parts of it to someone you need to forgive or ask forgiveness from, or someone you share a memory with or wish to encourage. Your spiritual journal benefits others when you share excerpts for the glory of God, in person or in writing. Everyone around you wins because all of you become better Christians.

While ordinary journaling might explore language or encourage you to increase your vocabulary, spiritual journaling gives you new words to express what God is doing in your life.

Journaling keeps your mind attentive to the present moment, providing a state of mindfulness that increases your happiness, but spiritual journaling increases your mindfulness of God. Because God is in the present moment, I visualize an oasis of peace where I stay close to the Source of all ideas and encouragement. He gives me much to write about from spiritual lessons learned in my everyday experiences, and much to share about his love and mercy as he heals me of many hurts of the past and calms my fears of the future.

Journaling can help you sketch out plans to achieve your dreams, but when you write down your goals in your spiritual journal, you allow room for God to steer you toward what he has planned for you.

Many people find that journaling increases their self-awareness by allowing them to sort out their feelings and helping them manage them. Writing through your experiences can build a "bridge of empathy" where you can meet others and understand what they are going through. In a spiritual journal, the Holy Spirit can enlighten this process and guide you to share bits of your own story to minister hope to others.

When you write down your experiences and aspirations, your brain and hand cooperate in composing and re-composing thoughts and ideas, bringing clarity to your story and improving your cognitive recall. In a spiritual journal, that improved clarity is enlightened by the Holy Spirit, who will then prompt you to share your recollections in spontaneous one-on-one conversations and public speaking.

Spiritual journaling exercises your spiritual muscle, growing holy habits that bring joy to every area of your being. Keeping a journal requires discipline and consistency for the best results. Like an athlete training for competition, to get good at it, you need to set aside a time each day or week to write in your journal, and then repeat the exercise frequently and regularly to build your "spiritual muscle." As you develop this holy habit, you'll find it comes easier, and the self-discipline you've acquired will spill over into other areas of your life.

And like regular exercise, journaling puts you on a path to emotional, physical, and psychological healing.

Putting your disordered thoughts into your spiritual journal clarifies them and frees you from the snarls of traumas that your mind replays. As you release your emotions during journaling, stress decreases and you sleep better in the peace of the Lord.

Want to jump-start your creativity? Try writing whatever comes into your stream of consciousness first thing in the morning. Julia Cameron introduced this practice in her book *The Artist's Way* as "morning pages," an excellent exercise to destroy writer's block and loosen up your brain to divulge ideas that will amaze you. In spiritual journaling, this exercise gives you the creative freedom to explore more deeply who you are in the Lord, so that you can discover all that God meant for you to become.

Research shows that, as you record the positive aspects of your life, journaling boosts your confidence by releasing endorphins and dopamine in your brain that elevate your self-esteem and mood. Spiritual journaling elevates your confidence in God's plan for your life and your ability to cooperate with his grace in all that he wants for you. Recording your faith story boosts your confidence by encouraging you as you explore what God is doing in your life and realize the many ways he loves you.

Journaling can heighten the joy of everything you do. When you place your thoughts and dreams, disappointments and dilemmas before the Lord, your journal becomes a spiritual journal.

Ask Yourself: How do I perceive that spiritual journaling will change my life for the better?

Best Practices for Keeping a Spiritual Journal

Remember, no one is looking over your shoulder critiquing what or how you write. Get lost in the experience of expressing yourself on paper in God's presence as he takes you through the puddles and over the rapids of the living river of your faith story.

You don't have to spend hours every day journaling. I don't. Sometimes all I can manage to do is a weekly update. But when I try to remember all the graces and blessings of the last few days, I know something important is missing. I've forgotten many irreplaceable moments because I did not take the time to journal.

Consistency in prayer journaling is more important than when and where. In fact, the spiritual guide and author Fr. Jacques Philippe writes in *Time for God* that we risk becoming discouraged if we take on more than we can handle when setting aside this time for God. He encourages us to begin with twenty minutes to half an hour each day, which is better than two hours now and then. The half hour each day you spend praying and journaling yields more spiritual growth than longer, more sporadic periods.

It's good to find a time and place with few distractions such as during adoration, or before or after Scripture study or daily Mass. Sometimes my computer is the worst place to journal. Although I may jot down a quick thought to explore later, invariably something pops up on my screen to distract me.

If you have tried journaling before and ended up in a "pity party of one," I encourage you to try again, this time with fewer self-expectations and more expectant faith that God is with you and will encourage you. Believe that he loves you unconditionally, share from your heart, and open it to his perfect will for you.

Perhaps you are concerned with protecting your privacy. You hesitate to share freely with God because you are afraid your scribblings will be revealed, exposing you to ridicule. I protect my notebooks from those who might not understand where I'm coming from, and leave the rest to God. My concern for privacy is one reason I prefer spiral notebooks—to tear out pages that I don't want to be around when I'm gone.

The blessings of spiritual journaling—to you and anyone who has grown closer to God because you shared from your spiritual journal—overwhelmingly outweigh the privacy risk.

The Blessings of Keeping a Spiritual Journal

When you open your heart and your journaling to the Holy Spirit, the floodgates of Heaven open. You will feel a downpour of wisdom, charity (love), understanding, counsel, fortitude, knowledge, piety, and fear of the Lord.

The fruits of the Spirit are perfections that the Holy Spirit forms in you as the first fruits of eternal glory. You become alive in the Spirit. Scientific research has shown that when you keep a journal regularly, your mind will be brighter, your recall sharper, your senses quicker, your self-discipline stronger, your communication clearer, your healing deeper, your creativity freer, your outlook brighter, your laughter louder, your stress calmer, your compassion greater, and your confidence higher.

As you begin to experience one or two of these fruits of the Spirit through your journaling, know that all of them don't come immediately. Enjoy and develop the ones that you detect. Anticipate more emerging, and thank God that ultimately they will fully bloom in Heaven.

Whatever format you may choose for your spiritual journal, the important thing is to keep your focus on writing about what God is doing in your life. Your spiritual journal may contain much about your non-spiritual activities, making the journal a place to connect everything you are and do with God. Maybe you identify what he is doing in your life as you record your prayers and his answers in a prayer journal. Here you can find clarity, guidance, healing, and comfort during hard and confusing times.

Your journal can be a running conversation with the Lord, building your relationship honestly, openly, and authentically. Talk to him as the best friend you will ever have. Tell him everything in your heart. Your secrets cannot shock him. He already understands the height and breadth and depth of what you are feeling, but you may not have a clue—until you have an "ah-ha" moment. Or see your tears splashed on the pages of your journal and feel his healing embrace of love.

You can call on the power of our Almighty Creator and trust him to help you sort everything out. As you write, ask him to help you sift through the silt to the bottom of the river of your story and decide what to keep and what to reject, what is real and what is fake, what separates the everlasting from the temporal wisp of the wind.

You can make any journal your spiritual journal by including God in what you write. Then you have a workbook to grow your spiritual life into a beautiful love relationship with God.

Ask Yourself: Can I imagine integrating spiritual journaling into my life? What blessings do I want that I can expect to receive by keeping a spiritual journal? How can these benefits contribute to my being able to share my Catholic faith story?

5

Know Your Story

I HAVE FOUND THAT faithfully keeping a spiritual journal keeps me always ready for any opportunity to share my conversion story and ready to convey the compassion and mercy of God to others.

To know our faith story, we need facts and clarity about our faith life so far. The tool of journaling is essential to being aware of our faith journey with God, bit by bit, as we live it. It also leads to a second tool: a *timeline of faith events.*

Create a timeline of faith events by jotting down in chronological order events of importance in your faith life. Certainly you can begin your timeline with or without years of journals to refresh your memory. You can break the timeline down into five-year periods. Perhaps start with your baptism and continue through the Sacraments you have received. In these and other significant events, note the high points, the holy moments that bubbled up and brought you closer to the Lord. Then contrast these moments with the moments of disappointment and disillusionment when you felt far from God.

What was that first defining moment when you knew that God was real, that he loved you? Mark that with a star. That's the most important experience. Focus on the God-moment that changed you.

Ask Yourself: What experience changed my life because of my encounter with Jesus Christ? Can I see myself sharing this experience?

What is Your Galilee Moment?

One approach that helps many people define the God-moment in their faith story is described in Pope Francis's homily on the Easter Vigil, 2014. He referred to Jesus after his Resurrection telling his disciples to return to Galilee where they first gave their lives to him. Jesus first proclaimed the Gospel in Galilee, and there he called the disciples:

> After John had been arrested, Jesus came to Galilee proclaiming the Gospel of God: "This is the time of fulfillment. The kingdom of God is at hand. Repent, and believe in the Gospel." As he passed by the Sea of Galilee, he saw Simon and his brother Andrew casting their nets into the sea; they were fishermen. Jesus said to them, "Come after me, and I will make you fishers of men." Then they abandoned their nets and followed him. (Mark 1:14–18)

After Jesus' death on the Cross, at what they thought was the end of everything they had hoped for, the angel in the Resurrection story instructs the followers of Jesus, reminding the women what Jesus wanted them all to do after his death:

> And entering the tomb, they saw a young man sitting on the right side, dressed in a white robe; and they were amazed. And he said to them, "Do not be amazed; you seek Jesus of Nazareth, who was crucified. He has risen, he is not here; see the place where they laid him. But go, tell his disciples and Peter that he is going before you to Galilee; there you will see him, as he told you." (Mark 16:5–7)

Pope Francis made two points with reference to these passages. First, "To return to Galilee means above all to return to that blazing light with which God's grace touched me at the start of the journey." To "return to Galilee" also means

> [Renewing] the experience of a personal encounter with Jesus Christ who called me to follow him and to share in his mission. . . . It means reviving the memory of that moment when his eyes met mine, the moment when he made me realize that he loved me.

Ask Yourself: What is my Galilee moment, where I first met the Lord and where I need to return?

Your Faith Bio

Continue taking your time to reflect on your faith journey: where it began, how it came alive and grew strong with difficulties, victories, and miracles. Take the timeline of faith events and create your "faith bio" by adding some details to those God-moments of closeness to the Lord. This faith bio is your resource for sharing your formal testimony. The faith bio will remind you of many treasured incidents to include in your formal testimony, times you also can share informally when prompted by the Holy Spirit. Select the highpoints according to how they brought you nearer to God.

You may have more than one God-moment, as you will later see that I did. Begin with the first encounter with Jesus that began your personal relationship with him, the moment you knew he was real and loved you personally. Fill in as much detail as you feel necessary to recreate it for sharing. Continue writing what you remember about subsequent faith events, as I do in describing my dive into Catholicism in the following chapter.

You are using journal entries and your timeline of faith events to write about the most significant spiritual events in your life. Keep in mind that the process of creating your faith bio is a continuing exploration of your relationship with God. With each episode, consider where God took you spiritually and where you believe he is leading you.

6

Three Components of Every Faith Story

YOUR FAITH STORY, as with every conversion, reversion, renewal, healing, and miracle story, has three components that answer these questions:

- Who were you before your conversion, reversion, renewal, healing, or miracle happened?
- What God-moment—or Galilee moment, as Pope Francis called it—changed you? Was it a tidal wave of love sweeping over you or an undercurrent of God's love swelling in your heart?
- Who are you now? How has your life changed?

I'll take you through my longer conversion story, using these three elements and answering these questions.

1. Who was I before my conversion?

I was baptized when I was one year old in my grandmother's Protestant church and grew up going to Sunday School, Vacation Bible School, and youth group. I sang in the choir and helped out in the nursery.

At fifteen, I quietly committed my life to Jesus at a mountaintop youth retreat. I remember still the smoky campfire, the prayers and songs we shared around it, and the youth minister directing us to spread out into the trees and think about our relationship with God. As I walked through the woods, I quietly sang the words William Young Fullerton wrote to the tune of Danny Boy, "I Cannot Tell." I found a grassy spot and sat down under a tree. The verses tell the story of Jesus' birth and death for our salvation, and the jubilation of his returning as the Savior of the world. For the first time, I recognized that the undercurrents within me signaled the presence of Jesus living in my heart. Speechless, I stopped singing my favorite hymn to focus on him.

He gently made known his life in me through the gift of unexplainable joy that gushed from deep within me and filled me up. At that moment I knew God was real and loved me personally as my Savior.

As his love swept through me, I knew he was the only one who loved me like no one else ever could. In that life-changing God-moment of joy, I was overwhelmed with love for Jesus and committed my life to him.

I returned to the campfire, holding in my heart this glorious secret between Jesus and me. When the youth minister asked us to share what we had experienced, no one said a word. Not even me. I sat stone still, my eyes down, waiting for the rush of emotion coloring my face to subside. I kept silent at the most important moment of my spiritual life, and for decades afterward—not because I didn't believe my experience of Jesus' love was real but because I wasn't ready to share it. I didn't know how.

A major test of our relationship came three years later when my father died suddenly. My mother was too heartbroken, my older sister too distraught, and my younger sister too shut-down emotionally to comfort me. Jesus alone comforted me, and I knew he would never fail me.

Just before my opportunity for conversion, I was nineteen years old, living at home, and studying at the university across town. When my father died, our family's relationship with the pastor and staff of our church, where I had volunteered all during high school and worked in the summer, grew closer.

2. What happened to me that led to my conversion?

For me, conversion came as a tidal wave of love, followed by a seeping undercurrent of how God wanted to change my life. The tidal wave was the sudden and absolute certainty that Phil was God's gift of love to me—and it swept over me before Phil realized I was the one for him. We resisted getting serious, but we were falling deeply in love. I wanted a man with a strong faith. The trouble was, Phil's strong faith was Catholic! Before he even proposed, I asked myself, "Can I marry in his church or should I just move on? Can I live without Phil or my church family?"

One turning point came when I struggled with how I would tell my mother that our plans for my wedding in our beloved church might never happen. I realized that I had made my choice. I wasn't choosing Phil over God, only over my dream of marrying a Protestant in the church I loved.

Love quickly changed everything in my life—except my relationship with God. You see, I would do just about anything for Phil, but I knew in my heart that worshiping God must be between God and me. Even though I wanted Phil and me to be united in one faith, I couldn't change the way I worshiped God that easily. Perhaps as we raised our children Catholic, I would become one, too. Perhaps like my father-in-law, I might remain Protestant, yet attend Mass with my family. My full commitment to the Catholic Church would have to come later, if ever. When I found that my conversion to the Catholic Church was neither required nor expected, Phil and I became engaged.

Our wedding plans, like a sudden whirlpool, surprised everybody and disturbed many. My mother insisted we meet with our pastor about our plans, out of respect for all he meant to our family. When we told him we were marrying in the cathedral down the street, the exasperation in his eyes startled me.

Fr. Andrew Burke, the pastor of the cathedral, gave us a talk on marriage preparation and I met with him for six lessons of instruction. This was the custom before Vatican II. He married us under the huge golden wings of the Holy Spirit in the cathedral, but without Mass. Somehow both families were pleased. I was twenty and Phil was twenty-two.

Another turn of the river came almost three years later. We were finishing our two years in the service and heading home with a toddler and an infant. Away from family pressure, I had chosen not to attend the services of my Protestant denomination. I spent those years in the service trying out the disciplines of the Catholic Church, which at that time meant no meat on Fridays and trying to follow the Latin Mass.

In the Catholic churches in the three ports where we were stationed, I marveled at the universality of the Church, the consistency of the liturgy and the instructions from three different priests. The third priest said, "Nancy, you know enough to become Catholic. When you go home, have the priest who married you baptize you."

That was the moment I knew I was ready, the culmination of three years of practicing and learning Catholicism. And I knew by the peace in my heart that I belonged in the Church. Our two sons were Catholic. It was time for me. When we returned home, Fr. Burke gave me the grand trifecta of Sacraments. He baptized me (conditionally), heard my first Confession, and gave me my First Eucharist in the cathedral under the golden wings of the Holy Spirit. What an afternoon!

3. Who am I now?

Now I am one of those faithful Catholics that I saw in Phil so many decades ago. I thank God and my mother for a solid Christian upbringing, which nurtured my personal relationship with Jesus. The tenets of faith that I learned and practiced in my childhood enabled me to leave that denomination but not my relationship with God. I didn't abandon my first beliefs, but added the fullness of truth to my childhood faith.

I'm sure that falling in love with Phil was the only way that God the Father could ever get me into the Catholic Church. He goes to any extreme to guide us into the joy he has for us. And I find great joy in belonging to the Catholic Church.

He gives us what we need and gift-wraps it in what we want. I wanted a strong Christian marriage. God wanted that for me—in the Catholic Church. So he wrapped it in an irresistible package and swept a tidal wave of love over me that was more forceful than my strong Protestant upbringing, the pressures of my family, and my resistance to marrying a Catholic.

I might have been happy as a Protestant married to a Catholic, like my father-in-law. But what joy it is to share the Eucharist and many ministries with my husband and children.

Ask Yourself: What one culminating God-moment comes to mind from this example for me to focus on in my faith story?

7

Five Tools for Stirring the Waters of Christian Testimony

LET ME GIVE a word of encouragement to those of you who hesitate to share your relationship with the Lord; then we will take up creating your formal testimony.

After my God-moment at the youth retreat when I committed my life to the Lord, I kept the joy of Jesus inside me, where I knew it was safe and real and hidden. I thought that if I shared this tender relationship, it might dissipate. Besides, as the hymn "I Cannot Tell" implies, I couldn't explain why Jesus came to earth, why he suffered and died for us, or how he will return in glory. I couldn't explain the magnitude of what Jesus meant to me any more than I could explain the grandeur of the surrounding mountains.

When I returned from the retreat, Mother asked if I enjoyed it. I smiled and told her I really did. Then I went to my room to be alone.

I didn't share the joy of that God-moment with her or anyone for decades. That moment with Jesus, and so many since has brought me such overpowering joy that I sought solitude to keep that secret joy within me. Our spirituality is intimate and personal; it's supposed to be private, right?

As I grew up in the Lord and other people shared their God-moments of conversion with me, I realized I was wrong. Yes, spirituality is personal, but it's not private. My "I Cannot Tell" chant is now "Always be ready." In 1 Peter 3:15, St. Peter opens a whole new viewpoint for hesitators like me, and perhaps you, when he writes, "Always be ready to give an explanation to anyone who asks you a reason for your hope" (NABRE).

This Scripture helped me wade into sharing my first moment of conversion with one or two people, then a small group. Now I collect conversion stories on my blog and tell my story to Catholic groups and conferences to help others share their faith stories.

We can wade safely into witnessing to those around us, perhaps like the youth minister and my mother, that sense that joy alive in our hearts. They don't push us to confess our conversion, because they love and respect us. But they know. And they want to know more. They want to listen to our story and find that joy we try to hide. It's okay to share with your family and friends.

Then look around and follow the lead of others who quietly or boldly take every opportunity to share the joy of Jesus that overflows from within their hearts. That joy is Jesus, the Word of Life that exists from the beginning and into eternity—and rushes forever through us into the hearts of others.

I cannot tell how or why Jesus lived and died the way he did. But this I know, he heals my broken heart, forgives my sins, calms my fears, and lifts me up because he is here with me now and always.

Before my birth, God inspired Fullerton to pen these words that still resonate in my heart today. He couldn't know how the hymn would impact my life and that of thousands, perhaps millions of Christians around the world. Long before that God inspired St. Peter to write the "Always be ready" Scripture that encourages me to evangelize. The Holy Spirit knew and provided these gifts well before he opened my heart to accept them.

In the same way, the Holy Spirit prepares us to share our stories by reminding us of poignant moments he has indelibly marked in our souls that can touch the hearts of others. Simultaneously, he is preparing the hearts of those we will encounter today, tomorrow, and next year.

Prompted by the Holy Spirit, we can wade into our river to find a little of our story to share, confident that God uses our witness however he wills. Our unique story may be their "I Cannot Tell" song, an "Always be ready" Scripture, or an unforgettable story that surges from the springs of faith within them. Our joy comes in the telling and the confidence that we are stirring the waters of faith in them into mighty waves that will break on other shores.

Your Formal Testimony

Now that you have a timeline and faith bio and know the three-part structure of faith stories, you are ready to compose your formal testimony.

Although it is the center part of your story, begin with your Galilee moment where you first came to know Jesus was real and loved you. Elaborate from your faith bio on the details of what happened in your encounter with Jesus. Was the experience dramatic or serene? Filled with conflict, then peace? Set the scene. Name the cast of characters. Enumerate the sequence of events. What happened to change you?

Then write the first paragraph, which will precede your Galilee moment. This shorter paragraph describes who you were before you enjoyed this life-changing experience with Jesus. Put your Galilee moment second. Conclude by describing the new you—who you are now and how your life has changed.

Your Elevator Speech

Remember to invite the Lord to spend time with you as you summarize your story. You'll know when you are ready to write a thirty-second elevator speech—a concise account you can give on the spot. This introduces the bare bones of your story to friends and strangers who show an interest in you as a Catholic Christian—perhaps someone who steps into an elevator with you or sits down next to you on a subway or airplane. This person may notice your crucifix or a Catholic book you are reading and begin a conversation about Catholicism. That's your signal to respond with a short summary of your faith story. Your unique story offers them a door they can open if they are interested in knowing more.

A brief telling of your conversion, adult commitment, return to the Church, healing, or answered prayer gets people interested faster than a long epistle. But don't try to share all of these events at once! Center your elevator speech around one event that sparkles on the river of your story to invite your listeners to wade deeper into it.

I didn't keep a spiritual journal as a young convert. But having journaled, made my timeline, used it to draft my faith bio, used that to write my formal testimony, and condensed it, I now can prepare a thirty-second elevator speech. I can sum up the essence of my faith story to answer anyone who asks me why I am Catholic. I have my elevator speech ready to stimulate interest in Catholicism in anyone I meet. To quickly test whether that person with me is interested in hearing more, I say:

> I grew up in a churchgoing Protestant family. I gave my life to the Lord at a youth retreat when I was fifteen. That God-moment carried me through the sudden loss of my father. I fell in love with a Catholic in college and married him in the Catholic Church. Almost three years later I converted to Catholicism, when I discovered I belong in the Catholic Church. That's where I can fully develop my relationship with God.

You don't need to memorize word-for-word the facts of your faith story or your elevator speech. Just spontaneously give the highlights of how you became Catholic, or why you returned to or remain in the Church. Be ready to elaborate, if asked, with details from your faith bio, always keeping focused on one event.

Let's review the five tools that create your faith story:

1. **Spiritual Journal**—a record of your experiences in your relationship with God where you interact with him, present your disappointments and victories, questions and frustrations to him, seeking his will for you. Journal time is a sacred time to find God within you and explore who you are in him. Your spiritual journal is an essential evangelization tool in building a timeline of faith, clarifying faith bio events, expanding details of your God-moments, summarizing your story in an elevator speech, and preparing to share your faith.
2. **Timeline of Faith Events**—bullet points of major events when you knew God was acting in your life. Determine (and mark with an asterisk) your first God-moment, if possible. This is a fluid document, added to in retrospect.
3. **Faith Biography**—notes with details on the timeline of faith events. Highlight and expand God-moments and surround them with supernatural

experiences of the strong presence of God such as healings, miracles, and answered prayer.

4. **Formal Testimony**—a written witness featuring your Galilee moment, organized as the center of the three components of faith stories.
5. **Elevator Speech**—a brief outline of relevant events before, during, and after your Galilee moment, and how that encounter with Jesus changed your life.

You can take this structure and build a collection of your faith experiences that come from the wellspring of your relationship with God and reveal a pattern of God's work in your life. The tools, with the three components and the concept of the Galilee moment, apply to every type of faith story. You can apply what you are learning here to every spiritual experience of a miracle, answered prayer, healing, renewal, or return to the Church. Giving voice to these faith episodes demonstrates to you and others how far nearer to him God has brought you since you began your spiritual journal.

Ask Yourself: How do these tools help me reflect on my relationship with God? How can I implement these tools to learn to share the love and mercy of God by sharing my faith story?

8

Lifetime Conversion

WHETHER YOU HAVE always been a faithful Catholic, have committed your life to the Lord as an adult, or converted to Catholicism, you probably have a story about renewing your faith. Renewal stories often are centered on inner healing. These are just as exciting and unpredictable as conversion stories.

Pope John Paul II teaches that conversion isn't a one-time event. We experience a step-by-step, continuous conversion during our lifetime. In *Familiaris Consortio* (*On the Role of the Christian Family in the Modern World*), he writes:

> What is needed is a continuous, permanent conversion which, while requiring an interior detachment from every evil and an adherence to good in its fullness, is brought about concretely in steps which lead us ever forward. (*Familiaris Consortio* 9)

When we recognize conversion as a lifelong calling, we can expect God to surprise us with little steps on flat stones in shallow water and high dives into cavernous pools that bring us closer to him.

Six years after my initial Sacraments, when I crossed over from Protestant to Catholic Land, Phil and I were Sunday Catholics, living in Dallas with four children. We prayed at Mass, before meals, at our children's bedtime, and when in need. Our two school-age children went to our parish school. We thought of ourselves as good Catholics, doing just fine. We looked like deeply devoted Catholics, but we were skimming the surface of authentic Catholicism. Sidetracked by worldly distractions, we were in danger of reducing our faith life to keeping up with the minimum requirements. We needed to take the next step in our continuous conversion.

Cursillo

God had something more for us—one of the renewal movements to revive our faith. We were invited to attend men and women's Cursillo. Those weekends expanded our spiritual vision for our family. We made close friends in our parish, and established new prayer habits.

Then we moved to the Boston area for three years when Phil became a member of the technical staff at the Massachusetts Institute of Technology. Soon we got lost in a huge overcrowded parish. During our last summer in Massachusetts, we attended Mass in a small church in a nearby suburb, where the Spirit-filled priest made the liturgy come alive. We loved it!

When we moved back to Dallas in the fall, we couldn't find that kind of parish atmosphere anywhere.

The parish in the neighborhood where we settled almost seemed dead. The religious education ministers struggled under the alcoholic pastor. To fulfill our duty to our children, my husband and I dragged our children and ourselves to Mass every Sunday.

We became disillusioned, and our marriage and family relationships deteriorated and almost bottomed out. With different agendas, the six of us competed for the family resources of time, money, and attention.

Life in the Spirit

Again, it took one of the renewal movements to snap us out of the self-involvement that was spiraling us apart. This time it was a Life in the Spirit Seminar that brought us into the fullness of Catholic community life during a time that few renewal opportunities existed. When the priest and lay people prayed over me for a new infilling of the Holy Spirit, a flood of emotion swirled around me. I landed in a place where I gave my life to the Lord—again, as I had on that mountain as a teenager more than twenty years earlier.

A fresh spring of joy flowed into my heart, opening a new way of life before me. I realized in a more mature way how God loves me—just the way I am, as no one else ever can. He was more real to me than I could express or imagine.

When I opened my eyes at the end of that prayer session, it was like the pivotal scene in the Wizard of Oz, when the tornado sets Auntie Em's farmhouse down and

Dorothy wakes up. As she opens the door to Oz, the scene slowly changes from black and white to Technicolor. Everything is brilliant. Dorothy experiences a new life she never imagined. That's what happened to me.

Phil and I dove into our new life in Christian community with Bible studies, share groups, and marriage enrichment. We got a new pastor and became Extraordinary Ministers of Holy Communion. We even began tithing.

Since then, many programs have sprung up on the diocesan or parish level that have nurtured our personal relationship with Jesus and invigorated our commitment to serve him in the Body of Christ.

Any parish mission, day of renewal, or retreat, any Advent, Lent, or summer program can bring you closer to Jesus than you ever imagined. Once, when I participated in a combination of parish programs and went to daily Mass, I experienced a profound awareness of the presence of God that spanned from Advent to Pentecost.

During that swell of the river, the joy of the Lord became alive—not just to endure but also to enjoy—wherever the winding river took me. I lived almost continually immersed in the joy of the Lord. He didn't take away my troubles, my physical problems, or my emotional struggles. He didn't remove disappointments and temptations. Rather his presence flooded everything around me and within me. He saturated me with an aura of joy. As I lived in his presence, Jesus became my joy.

This gift of enduring joy began with an Advent day of reflection, which prepared my spirit for a truly holy Christmas. The New Year gave me a fresh outlook. With new spiritual insight, I resolved to extend the holy joy of the season. An anniversary trip to San Diego dispelled the usual dreariness of January as the love of the Lord brought my husband and me closer.

Valentine's day took on a deeper meaning than romance. I applied passages from 1 Corinthians 13, on God's love, to a February publication I edited—and to my life. I took God's promise of unconditional love to heart. I wallowed in his love, as I had often wallowed in self-pity. It seemed that the joy of each day built on yesterday's high and promised a greater joy tomorrow as I lived in the presence of Jesus.

The joy of the Lord was my freedom during that Lent. Instead of giving up a certain food or habit, I gave up overcommitment. Instead of striving for more good works, I quietly rested in the Lord, spending as much time with him as possible. By Easter, every challenge in my life changed into a blessing, every relationship into a new treasure. Even when the joy of Easter faded, another upswing emerged. Our family celebrated Pentecost at an ecumenical worship service. Wow!

With this new attentiveness to joy, now, when I'm stuck in the mud and need courage or consolation, I can return to the memory of that season of joy. Since then I've suffered seasons of frustration and disappointment and endured heartbreaks I wasn't sure I would survive. But I never again felt alone, unloved, or rejected by the Lord.

The Lord's continual faithfulness to offer me ways to renew my love for him will never end. My joyful new life in the Spirit radically changed my life so that I can say without hesitation that I love Jesus and find him in the Catholic Church.

My renewed faith comes from a revitalization of my personal relationship with Jesus. Without it, I cannot become who God intends me to be. I cannot reflect his love in my unique personality. I cannot fulfill the mission of my baptism to evangelize, nor would I want to try.

Ask Yourself: Can I be open to a relationship with God that takes me to rocky places with hidden blessings?

9

Gentleness and Reverence: Tips for Sharing Your Faith Story

As you share the story of your conversion to the Catholic faith, your return to the Church, a healing, or a miracle, don't forget that your spiritual journal is your best tool for knowing your story. Keep your journal current. That's your resource for fresh material for new evangelization with its myriad and varied stories of little and big ways God showers you with mercy and love. Then you will "always be ready to give an explanation to anyone who asks you for a reason for your hope," but, as Peter adds, "do it with gentleness and reverence."

The "gentleness and reverence" Peter includes in his instructions are those viewpoints, attitudes, approaches, and people skills that make evangelization authentic when witnessing to Catholics or non-Catholics.

1. Be specific, not vague

Avoid generalities such as: "Let me tell you, God has blessed my life so much in every way. I just can never put it into words how he answered my prayers and brought me into the Church."

Instead, point out clearly what part God, prayer, or faith played in the experience. I might say, "As a faithful Protestant, God brought me a holy Catholic man to love and then brought me into the Church where I belong."

2. Speak in the listener's language

Avoid religious clichés and liturgical or theological terms. Tailor your words to the understanding and experience of your audience. Terms like "Eucharist" and "Mass" are foreign to many non-Catholics. Instead, talk about "Communion during our Sunday worship service." Later you can explain the theology of the terms. As for age appropriateness, I might tell my young granddaughter, "God loved me so much he brought me your Granddaddy to love so we could all be Catholic."

3. Speak with substance, not just with emotion

Tame emotional outbursts with the reality of the situation. Give the listener more nourishment than icing. I first submerged the emotional love story to highlight God's love. I didn't dramatize my struggles by telling how some relatives spoke against my marrying in the Catholic Church. Nor did I mention how, on Sunday, while still in our hometown before our tour in the service, I thought of my mother and sister down the street in the choir loft of the Protestant church singing some of the same hymns we were singing at Mass in the cathedral. Or the loneliness I felt during our military service when Phil was away at sea for months, and I, still a Protestant, went to Mass without him.

Let the listener remember the incident and how God resolved it without the splash-back of our pity party. Sharing our story is not about our dramatic surge to final victory, but about God's mercy. Resist the temptation to let emotions overwhelm what God did. Don't be like the lawyer who wrote on the side of his summation notes: "Your argument is weak here; shout louder."

4. Speak the truth

Do include failure, doubts, and inadequacies. Include high points and low points, but without the drama. Honestly tell how the experience taught you humility, perseverance, and God's faithfulness.

In my conversion story, I shared my sureness that God had sent me Phil to love. At the same time I was confused and frustrated as I struggled to clarify in my mind how I could abandon my denomination but not my relationship with God. The two flowed together, intricately intertwined.

State the problem, how long it lasted, how God resolved it, or helped you through it. Let his truth stand on its own.

5. Keep focused

You probably have many stories in your journal. Share the story of one incident that interests your audience—your conversion story, healing story, miracle story, or renewal story, but not all four. That's too much. Share only what they need to hear, without extra biographical details. Listen to the Holy Spirit. He will give you the most effective words on forgiveness, healing, prayer, love, the Eucharist, Reconciliation, or whatever they need the most.

(You can't imagine how I resisted the temptation to tell you about what "he said, she said" between me and Phil during the three years of my conversion.)

Wait for questions before telling more. Then share only what they ask.

Don't get sidetracked on tangents. It wasn't easy to keep focused on my conversion in the story of my romance, wedding, moving from home for the first time, and giving birth.

If those you are speaking with interrupt you to bring up something that has nothing to do with what you are telling, listen politely, answer quickly, then get back on track with your one topic. Time and attention spans are short. You want to leave them with one nugget of truth about God's love. What will you remember about my story? Receiving a trinity of Sacraments on that glorious Saturday afternoon? My extended season of joy? My Oz experience through Life in the Spirit?

6. Avoid self-righteousness

Don't imply that your path is *the* way and only way to experience God. Admit you don't have all the answers. Your listeners will respect you and what you say as they find their unique path.

How silly would it be for me to tell a Protestant woman to find a Catholic man to fall in love with so that she would then come to accept the Catholic Church? Or to insist to a returning Catholic that a renewal ministry is the only way to develop a personal relationship with Jesus?

Give the listeners the freedom to listen, ask questions, and share their doubts. Let them accept or reject your path to God. Then, in a silent prayer, set them free to find God's way for them.

7. Don't pick apart other people, churches, or ministries

The well-meaning Catholics who criticized my childhood church did not help me want to become Catholic like themselves.

The loving approach is positive, so find common values and spiritual truths to build on. We can all agree that we need God in our lives, that he loves us all, and that he has custom-designed a plan for each of us.

8. Stick to your part of the story

Let's not gossip or tell the stories of other people. That's not our job. Let them choose the time, place, and details they want to tell. Otherwise, who can trust us with their story?

Sticking to your part of the story applies to those *in* your story. Parts of my story are Phil's story, my mother's story, and my mother-in-law's story, but not mine to tell.

Your listeners need to know they can trust you more than they need to hear the graphic particulars of someone else's struggle.

9. Discreetly avoid sordid details

You are not telling your story in the confessional. Don't copy the old woman who confessed a sexual affair in her youth again and again. Finally, Father reassured her that God forgave her and she didn't have to keep confessing it. She replied, "I know, but I like to talk about it."

10. Relax. Speak matter-of-factly

You needn't draw back or speak aggressively because you are talking about a spiritual experience. You don't need to whisper as few words as possible as if you were at Adoration. You don't need to use a formal tone as if you were the lector reading Scripture. Use your one-of-a-kind voice for your one-of-a-kind story.

Ask Yourself: Which of these ten tips surprised me? Which one is the easiest to do? Which one is the hardest to accept?

10

Ways to Share Your Faith Story

SHARING OUR STORY does not require a theology degree, ordination, a formal public speaking platform, or even a highly visibly ministry. In *Evangelii Gaudium (The Joy of the Gospel)*, Pope Frances encourages us not to let lack of training stop us from evangelizing. But, he points out,

> Of course, all of us are called to mature in our work as evangelizers. We want to have better training, a deepening love, and a clearer witness to the Gospel. In this sense, we ought to let others be constantly evangelizing us. But this does not mean that we should postpone the evangelizing mission; rather, each of us should find ways to communicate Jesus wherever we are. All of us are called to offer others an explicit witness to the saving love of the Lord who, despite our imperfections, offers us his closeness, his word and his strength, and gives meaning to our lives. (121)

Conversion and renewal stories stir your heart as you marvel at how God makes miracles out of impossible situations. Just as your faith is built up by these stories, offering your conversion or renewal story encourages others tremendously.

But telling your story isn't only to encourage others. It encourages you because it's not just about *you*, but about what God is doing in your life. As scary as it seems at times, you're doing what God wants you to do: proclaiming the greatness of the Lord—and proclaiming it as only you can.

You can fill dozens of journals with anecdotes from your unique faith bio, blessing by blessing, as you welcome each gift the Holy Spirit reveals and prompts you to share at the ideal time and place.

Send your story to a Catholic website or magazine. Share your witness at Bible study, coffee breaks, family reunions, in airports, and waiting rooms—at every opportunity.

Condense your story into an arrow of love and then be ready for the target the Holy Spirit has prepared to receive it. Often you will find yourself with one person or a small group, hand-picked by the Holy Spirit. No coincidence there! An opening comes in the conversation just when the Holy Spirit nudges you to tell a significant incident in your faith story. A miracle. A healing. An answered prayer. You're on!

What to say? I've given you some guidelines for how to tell your faith story. But no one can instruct you on what to say—no one except the Holy Spirit. Jesus promised us in John 14:26 that "the Counselor, the Holy Spirit, whom the Father will send in my name, he will teach you all things, and bring to your remembrance all that

I have said to you." Jesus keeps his promises. The Holy Spirit will remind you of everything that Jesus has told you about your faith and your faith story. Then he will help you tell it.

Don't worry about your *ability* to share your story. God cares more about your *availability* than your ability. He's already there waiting for you. He set you up! Expect his presence to carry you through what you say and carry it beyond what you can ever imagine. His grace makes your story a tiny step or giant step in the spiritual life of someone else because you were available and allowed God to use you.

Start now with your spiritual journal. Dedicate some time to listening to the Holy Spirit. Let him reveal significant moments in the river of your faith story. Listen as he reminds you of the marvelous blessings God has brought to your life. He will help you unwrap the gifts he has hidden for you. Then, when the Holy Spirit surprises you with the ideal moment, you will "always be ready to give an explanation to anyone who asks you for a reason for your hope" (1 Peter 3:15-16, NABRE).

And now you know how to do it, "with gentleness and reverence."

Ask Yourself: Am I ready to begin to share my faith story and become the evangelist I was created to be? What might be holding me back?

Part 2

Testimonies:
Thirty Catholics Show You
How to Share Your Faith Story

Meet the Writers

THESE THIRTY CONTRIBUTING writers are faithful, enthusiastic Catholics serving the Church in faith formation, RCIA, Christ Renews His Parish, ACTS Ministry, Youth Ministry, Catholic Charismatic Renewal, Knights of Columbus, Marriage Encounter, and diocesan ministries. Many are Catholic schoolteachers and the faithful parishioners you will see as lectors, Extraordinary Ministers of Holy Communion, and willing volunteers.

In introducing them, I present these endearing friends who have inspired me with their faith stories. They have become my heroes, because they allowed God to transform them from their not-so-inspiring beginnings and put them on the sure path to Heaven—and they stepped out in faith and shared their testimonies. If you met them today, they would appear to have their act together, but they have all struggled—and have become victorious. You may be surprised to know that:

Julie Davis was an atheist who made a bargain with God.

Virginia Pillars brought her schizophrenic daughter home for a weekend that lasted four years.

Bill Alexander's alcoholic father, poor upbringing, and dyslexia convinced him as a child that God couldn't love him.

Rob Brull had to lose his parents, his savings, and his job before he got fired up about his faith through Catholic radio.

Cynthia Gill Bates left the Mormon Church of her childhood and found that Mormons make good Catholics. She gives us a thorough education on Mormonism.

Michael Fraley was an Evangelical who knew he needed something more and searched for Truth in the early Church Fathers.

Tima Borges had a troubled marriage that left God out of family planning.

Cheryl Ann Wills was a suicidal flower child headed for an early death.

John Chomistek had visits from God, who warned him about an impending disaster.

Bishop Mark Seitz experienced a moment of grace the summer he was eight that convinced him to become a priest.

Gloria Castro's Baptist neighbor led her through the Sinner's Prayer when Gloria was eighteen.

Bob Kurland, a physicist and secular Jew married to a Catholic, was drafted as an altar server at his daughter's baptism.

Jeannie Ewing questioned her Catholic faith in high school and bargained with her parents so she could go church shopping.

Elizabeth Reardon discovered in college that she no longer felt Christ's presence in her Protestant worship service.

Lisa Nicholas first saw a crucifix at a neighbor's home when she was in the first grade, but Lisa's mother told her it was nonsense.

Karl Erickson stood out as a Protestant in Catholic school and once was pulled out of the Communion line by a teacher.

Greg Wasinski had zero respect for the Real Presence of Jesus Christ in the Eucharist, until it became the point of his return to Catholicism.

Cyndi Lucky found out that, by allowing her to be adopted, God saved her from abortion and from being raised by an alcoholic, unwed mother.

Colleen Spiro found that the symbol of Jesus in the Protestant Communion service was not enough for her.

Neil Combs' Cursillo weekend began a three-year journey to learn about prayer and write a book on developing a deep relationship with Christ.

Sister Anne Marie Walsh, SOLT, had to experience death in a relationship to understand she was never going to find what she was looking for on a purely human level.

Diane Roe felt a big, comforting hug engulfing her as she slept; the storm ceased, and a familiar presence stayed with her.

Jennifer Fitz discovered just how far she had wandered from God when she entered a mission church and could not feel God's presence.

Margaret Reveira committed her life to Christ and immediately was attacked by her nondenominational friends, who insisted she could not be blessed unless she left the Catholic Church.

Lyn Mettler was a New Ager looking for self-improvement when suddenly she was given the eyes of faith, as if a light switch had been flipped on.

Virginia Lieto was a lukewarm Catholic, running through the motions of doing what was expected, when she felt drawn into a deeper commitment.

Brian Gill didn't want to become a Catholic, but what he learned in *Humanae Vitae* forced him to admit the truth.

Melanie Jean Juneau's Evangelical friend in high school stirred a yearning in her for deeper intimacy with God, but she did not know how to nurture it.

Kevin Luksus felt like he was in a hole; he wanted to get out, but he just didn't know how.

Enjoy getting to know these Catholics through their unique stories. Without knowing you, their testimonies can evangelize you and give you hope. Are you ready?

From Atheist to Happy Catholic

Julie Davis

My parents are atheists, so there was no religion in our home. They never tried to prejudice us against religion; they just never talked about it. It was kind of like talking about sex—it was the unspoken rule that you just didn't mention religion.

As issues came up, we were taught to be good people in the morality of popular culture: work hard and do your best, be honest, don't steal, cheat, or lie. We learned that a lot of other issues were all relative. As long as you didn't hurt other people or break the law, what you did was your own business.

Of course, even though they never talked about religion, we all knew that those boring churchgoers were weak because they needed a crutch like religion to get by.

Early in our married life, neither Tom nor I gave God much thought. We were just living our lives. And then God used what we cared about most to get our attention.

Hannah's Assignment

The oldest of our two daughters, Hannah, had a terrible teacher in public school and nothing we tried solved the problem. So, halfway through kindergarten, we switched her to St. Thomas Aquinas Catholic School. Her religion teacher asked all the kids which of them went to Mass every Sunday. Almost all the kids raised their hands. Hannah didn't. Mrs. McDaniel told those children that they needed to go home and tell their parents that they should be going to Mass every week. Dutifully Hannah passed the message. There is no one for knowing black from white and "yes" from "no" like a kindergartener. She didn't buy our feeble excuses and started quoting her religion lessons to us. Pretty soon we were attending weekly Mass at St. Thomas.

Tom was Catholic, but he hadn't attended church in a long time. I wasn't even sure if there was a God. How are you ever really sure? Most of the "proof" anyone ever offered seemed an awful lot like a coincidence to me. But, I couldn't sit there week after week listening to Father B. without starting to wonder . . . is there a God or not?

Let's Make a Deal

I was so clever, I figured out a sure-fire way to find out. (I'll just say here that I am thankful God protects fools because, looking back, I can't believe I had such nerve!) About a year before, we had tried everything to sell our house. Even though the realtor said everything was just right and there should have been no problem, no one would even make an offer. So, kneeling at Mass one day, I made God a deal. All he had to do was to get me a new house, as a sign. Then I'd know he was there . . . *and* I'd have a new house.

Of course, nothing happened. Except that, because I had made that deal, I found myself listening more carefully at Mass and thinking even more. After about a year went by, one Sunday when we were kneeling at Mass, I told God the deal was off. I didn't need proof. It wasn't because of any dramatic feeling or discovery. I just didn't have a reason not to believe anymore, so I went ahead and took his existence on faith.

Unexpected Refund

That week our new accountant found major errors in the past three years' taxes that gave us a huge refund—$11,000—enough for a down payment on a new house, new furniture, and some remodeling. In a time when houses were sold within days of going on the market, we found a house that had been sitting on the market for months for no apparent reason, except that it was perfect for us and the price had just been lowered to exactly the amount we could afford.

Two weeks after that, our own house sold, without ever going on the market, to a girl who was determined to have a house with our exact specifications, within a specific six-block area. We were right in the middle of that area. All the realtors and the people at the title company individually marveled at how smooth and fast things went on the sale of our old house and the purchase of our new one. They all said they had never seen anything like it.

I don't believe in coincidence anymore.

Becoming a Happy Catholic

Now I had faith, but I didn't see any reason to become Catholic. Hannah and Rose received their First Communions, and Tom went to Confession and started receiving Communion again. I didn't mind sitting in the pew until they got back. But, over time, whenever everyone went for Communion, I developed a yearning for the Eucharist that became an actual physical ache. This went on for months. A few weeks before Easter, I decided I'd better find out how to become Catholic, because I couldn't stand it any more.

I couldn't believe it when I found out I would have to wait about a year before completing the Rite of Christian Initiation for Adults (RCIA) and entering the Church the next Easter. That was the longest year of my life, although I found RCIA to be an interesting spiritual journey in itself, which I had not expected. I think it is funny that I am such a reader (and have been my whole life) but God chose to reach me in a way that was totally outside books at all.

Finally, it was the Easter Vigil of 2000, the wonderful day when I became Catholic and could receive the Eucharist. I love it. I love the traditions, I love the saints,

I love the Eucharist . . . I love being Catholic. (That was about six years after I told God I believed in him.)

How God Used My Conversion

And God blessed me that day in a way that I will never forget.

When I was kneeling after Communion, I felt a tap on my shoulder and looked up to see my father-in-law smiling at me as he walked toward the altar. He had not been to Communion since the 1960s when Vatican II changes made him so mad that he turned his back on the Church altogether. Tom's devout mother and his aunts had been praying for many, many years for his return to the faith, so I was thrilled to see him receive Communion. His sister, Tom's aunt, was my sponsor and she hissed in my ear, "Has he been to Confession?" I was so happy I just said, "That's between him and God. Let it go."

Later Tom's mother said that my father-in-law told her that if I had decided to become Catholic, it was because I had thought about it thoroughly and knew it was the right thing to do. That was when he decided to come back to the Church. And, yes, he had been to Confession. He had carefully planned to have his return to Communion be at my Confirmation. He had gone before they left Houston. For my father-in-law to show such total respect for my decision to become Catholic by rethinking his faith was overwhelming. Even more overwhelming was the realization that God had used my conversion not just for my good but also to reach someone close to me—and I had been unaware of it.

The Power of Conversion

One of the things that made my conversion so powerful to me in retrospect is that it was done without any reading or influence from outsiders at all. This was all just between God and me. No one else's opinion was even solicited, as I really didn't talk about that sort of thing. (I know a bunch of people probably wish I were *still* that way!)

One of my Confirmation gifts was a book by Scott Hahn that started me down a whole new path of reading. I had no idea anyone wrote books about this stuff! I devoured Scott Hahn, Peter Kreeft, Francis Sheed, books about the saints, everything I could get my hands on . . . and so on to the Christ Renews His Parish (CRHP) retreat and so on to *Happy Catholic* . . . and here I am today, waiting to see where he's gonna take me next on this wild, but very interesting ride.

Julie Davis, *graphic artist and author, is the daughter of atheists but always seeking. She is not always happy but always happy to be Catholic. She blogs at Happy Catholic and Meanwhile, Back in the Kitchen, and podcasts novels at Forgotten Classics. Her latest of several books is* Seeking Jesus in Everyday Life.

Broken Brain, Fortified Faith

Virginia Pillars

I AM A "cradle Catholic." My family and both sets of grandparents attended the same Catholic parish. My first outing after birth was to church where I received the Sacrament of Baptism.

I grew up in a large farm family with eight brothers and two surviving sisters. For many years, at least one of us occupied a desk at our parish grade school. Before I reached puberty, I'd received the Sacraments of Confession, First Holy Communion, and Confirmation. Saturday afternoon trips to the confessional, along with weekly Sunday Mass, were part of our routine.

In 1975, I stood next to Roy, a Catholic boy from a neighboring farm community, and we received the Sacrament of Matrimony. Together we raised four children as we built our farming operation to a comfortable level. I guess to many around us we may have seemed like the ideal Catholic farm family. And if I'm honest with myself, I felt that life had treated us well.

I felt blessed. Until late 2004, when our life changed almost overnight.

Faith Challenge

Our life deteriorated daily at an alarming rate. Chaos seemed to close in from all sides. We went from what I perceived as a "normal" life for our family into one that made little sense. And I had to find a new path for my faith journey that challenged, educated, and humbled me more than I ever dreamed was possible.

On December 9, 2004, at my suggestion, our daughter Amber came home for the weekend. At age twenty-four, she had a college degree and a full-time job as a youth minister in a town about sixty miles away, but during the past months I had witnessed a change in her. She seemed to have lost her zest for life. She assured me that she had things under control. That day her employer, who was disturbed by Amber's behavior, called me. I called Amber and, after hearing her sobs over the phone, I shared her employer's concerns. I raced to her apartment at ninety miles per hour and brought her home for what I thought would be a long weekend.

Those three days morphed into weeks. During that time, her brain broke, and we no longer shared the same reality. Memories, fears, and imagined sights and sounds melded into a frightening world for her. Nothing we said could convince her that these things were not happening. She seemed trapped in her mind, a place that included a conspiracy to kill her.

Even with my large family and circle of close friends, I had never felt more alone in my life. I didn't know where to turn for help. The Christmas season that year was anything but joyful. During a family party, Amber lashed out at her sister-in-law, completely unprovoked. We knew she needed help, but didn't know what to do. We'd tried hospitalization, but she checked herself out again. We tried medication, but she eventually refused to take most of it. Roy and I realized that this situation was beyond our understanding, but we were at a loss on what to try next.

Abandoned

Desperation, fear, anxiety, and confusion all combined into the feeling that God had abandoned me. My faith hit the wall of uncertainty. The faith that I had carried all my life seemed far away. Sure, I still punched the proverbial time clock as I physically made my appearance at Sunday Mass. I recited the prayers and received the Eucharist, but in reality, I just clocked in and clocked out, nothing more. Nothing to take home with me. Nothing that I felt sustained me for what I faced within the walls of my home. I fulfilled my Sunday obligation, period. I felt alone, scared, and angry with God. Prayers and readings had no meaning for me and I stopped attending Mass . . .

. . . until I learned of a group of wonderful people who pulled me into their circle of friendship of caring and guidance. I found NAMI, the National Alliance on Mental Illness, an organization of individuals banded together to improve the lives of those living with mental illness. They supported me, a stranger, and helped me begin my journey to a new "normal."

At their encouragement, I shared our situation with our families and my closest friends. Additional support arrived in the form of notes, letters, and faxes with the promise of prayers for us, as well as stories of their experiences. It strengthened me.

I realized I needed to address both mind and spirit to face this Goliath of fear. I inhaled several books that taught me about the brain and what happens to it during mental illness. I tucked the lessons about how to manage and cope into my arsenal of defense. I returned to daily devotional reading and prayer, and listened to songs of faith. Sometimes I kept the house silent as I worked, while I talked out my frustrations and worries to God. Through this, I realized that God hadn't chosen Amber and said, "I give you schizophrenia." I went from "Why are you doing this?" to "What should I do?" During prayer, ideas came to me on how to cope, how to improve our situation, and what to do next.

Still, we watched in agony as schizophrenia unleashed the many nasty symptoms it had to offer. Medicine didn't work, and Amber's symptoms worsened at an alarming rate. I asked my family and friends to join me in three specific prayer requests: that the doctors would find the right cocktail of medication to help Amber; that she would understand her illness; and that I would find wisdom and understanding.

Amber's Breakthrough

The doctors tried different medications and increased dosages, which led to a horrific dystonic reaction for Amber. She lost control of her muscles as they stiffened and convulsed. Through those terrifying moments, Amber had a breakthrough. The medication that lessened the reaction became the catalyst for her to understand her illness. She realized her need for medicine and her healing began. The process was slow, filled with disappointment and frustration, but it also assured me that God had not abandoned me.

Upon Amber's release from hospital care to our home, ideas to retrain her brain came to me during morning devotion time. Brain games became part of our daily routine, along with creating an environment for her to heal. I managed her medications and treated her as though she'd come home after cancer treatments. I let her decide when to sleep, how much to eat and how to spend her time. We watched her health improve with tiny steps forward, back, and then forward again.

In 2004, I brought my daughter home for a weekend that lasted four years. During those years, healing occurred, both for Amber and for me. Now I look at my daughter Amber and see a miracle. I look back over the past twelve years and see the hand of God at work—the gift of healing. During those years, Amber worked to regain her health. Today, she understands her illness—there is no cure, but with medication and the proper lifestyle she can manage it. She works full-time, lives in her own apartment, manages all her finances and affairs, and leads an active social life. Best of all, she remains devoted to God.

I came to understand that the many avenues of support I received from those around me were an extension of God's love and care. Family and friends acted as God's hands. Each letter, card, and love in action bolstered my spirit. Through them, God answered my pleas for help.

Today, I no longer just punch a clock each time I attend Mass. It's a time of worship. The prayers and the song lyrics help to renew, fortify, and strengthen me as I go. I relish my morning devotional reading and prayer time.

Now, I share our story and hope—that recovery is possible. I also volunteer for the NAMI organization to support other families that deal with mental illness, where I teach a class for families and lead support groups. I want to allow God's love and mercy to flow to them as it flowed to me. If I can be that vessel for others, it gives my experiences meaning and glorifies God.

***Virginia Pillars** is an author, speaker, and mental health volunteer. Her book,* Broken Brain, Fortified Faith: Lessons of Hope Through a Child's Mental Illness, *won the 2017 Selah Award for Memoir and the CWG Seal of Approval. She has contributed to* Grief Diaries: Poetry, Prose and More *and The Mighty online community. She blogs at www.virginiapillars.com.*

Saved by Don Quixote

Bill Alexander

I GREW UP IN southern New Jersey, the fourth child of six. My parents were Protestants. I was baptized in the Methodist church at the age of thirteen and had very little religious training. We were a dysfunctional family because my father was an alcoholic. I reacted to his drinking in numerous ways. I became aware of the way we lived—not having the proper necessities. In other words, I had long hair and holes in the knees of my pants, long before they were fashionable. I always felt that we were from "the other side of the tracks." I related socially by becoming shy, backward, and insecure.

Our way of life also affected me in the way that I related to God. I knew there was a God out there somewhere, but I didn't know him. I missed a great deal of school in my early years, was labeled a slow learner and got pushed from grade to grade. When I left school, I was barely able to read or write. Many years later, I found that I had a learning disability: dyslexia.

New Jersey is the second most populated Catholic state, and many of my friends were Catholic. One of my best friends was the president of the Catholic Youth Organization (CYO). I played CYO sports and attended CYO dances. I even attended a few Confraternity of Christian Doctrine (CCD) classes. I didn't learn very much. I only went because that's where all the pretty girls were. The priest was the youth director, and he befriended me. He was always encouraging and seemed concerned and interested. He didn't preach to me about becoming Catholic; he was just a witness to me.

I first met Deana at a CYO dance several years before we began to date. She invited me to attend Mass with her. Every time I went to Mass with her, I experienced this special presence of God, which I would come to understand several years later.

As we continued our relationship, Deana had the good sense to pray about God's will in her life. I had never met a girl like that. I was impressed with her witness. We dated for almost a year and married on May 19, 1962. I continued to go to Mass with her. Three years later, I became a Catholic. I was really enthusiastic—I was going to be the best Catholic that I could be.

After a few years, I became a Catholic in name only. I had a lot of misconceptions about God. I could not conceive that the God of the whole universe loved me, nor did I know that he wanted a personal relationship with me. I was told that he loved me, but I never experienced that love. After ten years, our marriage became a rocky road. By now we had five children and I was working two jobs to make ends meet. I complained a lot, was irritated and frustrated.

In February 1972, my job with American Airlines in Philadelphia became shaky. I feared I would be laid off. In March we came to Dallas to look around. We knew about the new airport, which would give me job security. We liked what we saw and put in for a transfer.

At that same time, in February 1972, we signed up for a Marriage Encounter retreat weekend, which we made in April of that year. God was truly present to us. He touched me on that weekend in a profound way. I experienced his love for the very first time. It was so profound that I could give you the exact date, time, and place.

Here's what happened: After the first session on Friday evening, Father Murray told us that he would be available for Confession until midnight. Deana and I decided to go to Confession as a couple. It was the first time that we had gone to Confession with a priest, face-to-face. After this experience, the Lord greatly blessed us.

The retreat just got better from there. Saturday morning, the first session was "Encounter with Self." After the presentation, the retreat team played music from the Broadway show, *Man of La Mancha*. For me, it was like a personal parable of God's love. Through it, I saw myself as a miserable sinner.

In this beautiful story, Don Quixote befriends a woman known as Aldonza, who was filled with shame because of her past life. She seethed with self-hatred and remorse. She cries out, "God, won't you look at me? . . . Born on a dung heap to die on a dung heap, a strumpet men use and forget!"

Then Don Quixote befriends her, bringing life, hope, purpose, and self-respect. He calls her his sweet lady. He gives her the endearing name Dulcinea. I saw in this the life-giving power of Jesus, restoring my worth, respect, and dignity and giving me newness of life.

The whole scene ends with the beautiful words:

To dream the impossible dream,
To fight the unbeatable foe . . .
To right the unrightable wrong . . .

After this experience, Jesus had me! I was his. He just engulfed me with his unconditional love and mercy. After that, I was hugging everyone in sight.

We were asked to be involved with Marriage Encounter and became a presenting couple. The job transfer came through and, when we moved to Dallas, we were a part of the first Marriage Encounter in North Texas.

Bill Alexander *came to Texas in 1972 to work for American Airlines. Now retired, Bill has a rich life with his wife Deana, seven children, eleven grandchildren, and eight great-grandchildren. The couple was involved in Marriage Encounter and share their faith teaching and facilitating Life in the Spirit and formation seminars.*

God's Catholic Answers

Rob Brull

FAITH WAS JUST a way of life while I was growing up in a devout Catholic family. Mom was the spiritual head of the household, dedicated to praying the rosary herself and making sure all in the family participated in the Sacraments. Dad was a little bit laxer in the rules of the Church but fully supported Mom in making sure we did what we were supposed to do.

As seems typical of many of my generation, when I went off to college I drifted away from my faith. The Evil One convinced me I did not need my foundation of faith anymore. These were new and exciting times. I had secular goals to strive for: wealth, success, and, most of all, impressing those around me.

Throughout my twenties, the only time I went to Mass was when Mom and Dad were coming to visit or when I went home to visit them. In my early thirties, God sent someone to me. A friend-of-a-friend asked if I would accompany them to church for Easter Mass, because they wanted to go but did not want to go alone.

While I never accompanied them to church again, after that one trip I felt drawn to attend each week. This incident began a decade of attending Mass weekly but not doing much else. Getting me to Mass was the first step in God's molding me.

While I was attending Mass in my thirties, I remember a gentleman from Catholic radio visiting the church, who encouraged us to tune into the new Catholic radio station. At times on my way home from work, if I was bored with sports talk radio and other news talk radio, I would tune in to the Catholic radio station. *Catholic Answers* was the show being broadcast, and they talked mostly about the interpretation of different verses of the Bible. But I was Catholic and thus considered the readings at church to be more than sufficient for what I needed to know about the Bible. However, God was planting a seed by nudging me to consider a deeper faith.

In my early forties, I hit the most trying times of my life. I experienced the death of both of my parents, lost a long-time job, and had a considerable amount of savings tied up in a real estate market that continued to plummet. Also, my oldest son could not attend pre-K4 because of disabilities related to fine and gross motor skills, and my marriage was probably not as good as it had been. At this point, God finally had my attention, and I was ready to let him mold me further.

I lost my job and, in his infinite wisdom, God gave me a much longer commute to work for my new job. He then led me to inspirational radio personalities who fired me up about my faith. Through these radio personalities, God convinced me that the answers to my struggles were not in the secular world, but in prayer. After a while, I even started looking forward to my drive home in traffic so that I could learn more about the Bible from *Catholic Answers.*

I ended up going to Confession for the first time in twenty-three years. I also bought my first Bible. Reading through it completely took almost a year as I contemplated so many things along the way. I continue to read through the Bible every day. It is part of our family bedtime routine along with the rosary, which I can still envision my mom praying when I was young.

These difficulties of my early forties seem so long ago now, even though it has only been a few years. Today has its own challenges, but I have such a different perspective knowing that I do not face them alone. I rely on the intercession of the saints and the love and mercy of our Heavenly Father and his Son.

The molding of my new self continues to take shape, and always will, as I strive to understand God's will for me today and for the future.

***Rob Brull** is a member of St. Thomas Aquinas parish in Dallas, Texas. Rob and his wife Sara have four children. He participates in pro-life activities and enjoys teaching the faith to his children. An electrical engineer by training, he works as a product manager in the healthcare industry.*

Mormons Make Great Catholics

Cynthia Gill Bates

I WAS BORN IN San Antonio, Texas, and lived there until I was sixteen years old. We lived a few blocks from St. Thomas More parish and school, and many of my neighbors attended school there. My father spent his career as Chief Financial Officer at several Catholic hospitals in Texas and Colorado. I remember visiting the motherhouse of the Benedictine sisters who owned the nursing home and hospital where my father worked in San Antonio, and even attending Masses there when I was very young.

My parents raised me as a member of the Church of Jesus Christ of Latter-Day Saints, better known as the LDS Church or Mormon Church. I was raised a TBM ("True Believing Mormon"), devoutly practicing the faith from the time I was very young until my college years. My parents converted to Mormonism when I was a baby, or maybe right before I was born. My uncle—my father's brother—had converted, and my father and family converted shortly after that.

Growing up Mormon allowed me to experience my teenage years in a safe and secure environment. While our family had periods of being considered "inactive" (infrequent attendance at Sunday church services), for the most part, we went to church every week. I was baptized on my eighth birthday, which I remember being a very special honor. My parents were "sealed" to each other and to my younger brother and me during my junior year of high school in the Dallas, TX, Temple. I participated in many of the milestones of Mormon youth and adolescence, such as Scripture-chasing during my early-morning seminary classes and singing in roadshows (although I was never lucky enough to perform in "My Turn on Earth" or "Saturday's Warrior").

When I was in college, I started dating a nice young man who didn't have a religious upbringing. When we started dating, I made it clear how important my beliefs were to me. He read the Book of Mormon from cover to cover and was baptized, and we continued to date for two and a half years.

It Began with a Book

In the spring of 1992, my boyfriend and I were in a bookstore near a mall in East Texas. I was looking at religion books and was inspired to pick up an "anti-Mormon" book. I can't remember what shocking revelation in this book made me want to buy it. I just remember that I read something that was convincing enough for me to leave the religion I had believed my entire life.

Here's the secret of what happens when a Mormon leaves the church: When faith in Joseph Smith is lost, all faith in the truthfulness of the Mormon religion goes, too.

Everything in the entire religion revolves around the teachings and doctrines of the founder of the Mormon religion, Joseph Smith.

In a sermon called "The Cornerstones of Our Faith," Gordon B. Hinckley, a modern-day leader of the Mormon Church, described this concept well:

> These great God-given gifts are the unshakable cornerstones which anchor the Church of Jesus Christ of Latter-Day Saints, as well as the individual testimonies and convictions of its members: (1) the reality and the divinity of the Lord Jesus Christ as the Son of God; (2) the sublime vision given the Prophet Joseph Smith of the Father and the Son, ushering in the dispensation of the fullness of times; (3) the Book of Mormon as the word of God speaking in declaration of the divinity of the Savior; and (4) the priesthood of God divinely conferred to be exercised in righteousness for the blessing of our Father's children.

Joseph Smith and the Book of Mormon are the cornerstones of the Mormon religion. Take those away, and everything else crumbles. There are only two possible options: either Joseph Smith told the truth, or Joseph Smith lied. Either Joseph was visited by God the Father and Jesus Christ, or he was not. Either the Book of Mormon is what it claims to be, or it is not. Period.

My boyfriend and I left the church at the same time. Our calling at the time (a volunteer position assigned by church leadership) was teaching a Primary class. We simply called the church and said we could no longer teach the class and that we would no longer be going to the Mormon Church. We broke up about four months later.

RCIA, Round One

After leaving the Mormon Church in 1992, I briefly started going to the Catholic Church and attending RCIA classes. For a reason that has escaped me at the moment, probably something to do with college parties and other typical co-ed shenanigans, my Catholic catechesis didn't last for very long. I do remember buying my first rosary, a rosary that I still keep on my bedside table. After college, I became a religious agnostic for many years.

When I turned twenty-seven, I decided to give the Mormon Church one more try. I wanted to make sure I did everything I could to draw closer to God and find out if the Mormon Church really was what it claimed to be. I lived my late twenties as an active member of a Singles Ward (similar to a personal parish, for young single adults ages eighteen to thirty), but after years of not finding the answers I was seeking, I left the Mormon Church for the last time. Soon after I left the Mormon Church for good, in 2001, I met my husband. We were engaged nine months after we met and were married six months after that. As a married couple before my conversion to the Catholic faith, we attended church together only about a dozen times. We attended the Mormon Church with my parents at their home Ward, and we also went to a couple of Catholic weddings. We tried a Unitarian church once, but that didn't work for either of us.

In October 2005, my husband and I went to the Catholic wedding of one of our neighbors. I remember that, while sitting in the beautiful little church, I was so jealous of people who received the Eucharist. I wanted to experience that. I felt this warmth, this serenity sitting there in the chapel. And then, as God worked within me, switches started getting flipped in my head. I realized that I could do this: I could be Catholic. I could get baptized if I wanted. I could go to a Catholic church *every week* if I wanted, or even every day! I could be a part of this.

Two weeks later, I was in RCIA. Although I had been baptized as a Mormon, the Catholic Church regards Mormon baptisms as invalid. Joseph Smith taught that:

> It is the first principle of the Gospel to know for a certainty the character of God, and to know that we may converse with him as one man converses with another, and that he was once a man like us: yea, that God himself, the Father of us all, dwelt on an earth, the same as Jesus Christ himself did . . . God himself was once as we are now, and is an exalted man, and sits enthroned in yonder heavens! . . . In the beginning, the head of the Gods called a council of the Gods; and they came together and concocted [prepared] a plan to create the world and people it. When we begin to

> learn this way, we begin to learn the only true God. ("The King Follett Discourse")

Although in a Mormon baptism the Trinitarian formula is recited, the Father, the Son and the Holy Spirit in the teachings of the Latter-day Saints:

> are not the three persons in which subsists the one Godhead, but three gods who form one divinity. One is different from the other, even though they exist in perfect harmony" (*L'Osservatore Romano*, Weekly Edition in English, Aug. 1, 2001, 4).

For this reason, I was not simply received into the Catholic Church, but baptized on Easter Sunday, 2006.

The Graces of Our Eucharistic Lord

During my conversion process, I participated in a lot of online forums. Many times, Mormons trying to convince me to come back to the Mormon Church contacted me. The following exchange between one such Mormon and shows the profound love of our Eucharistic Lord that I had experienced in my conversion. I wrote this two weeks before my baptism:

> **Mormon:** It's too bad you didn't take prayer seriously when you were a member of the true church. If you had taken Moroni's challenge and prayed "with real intent," you wouldn't have taken the path you are currently on. But, prayer in any context is good. So best wishes.
>
> **Me:** I want to make one thing perfectly clear. I begged, I pleaded, I cried for an answer to whether the Mormon Church was true. I prayed and begged for the simple

answer promised in Moroni [from the *Book of Mormon*]. You know the one:

> Moroni 10:4: And when ye shall receive these things, I would exhort you that ye would ask God, the Eternal Father, in the name of Christ, if these things are not true; and if ye shall ask with a sincere heart, with real intent, having faith in Christ, he will manifest the truth of it unto you, by the power of the Holy Ghost.

This is one of the very first scriptures that Mormon missionaries share with investigators. Pray for the truthfulness, and you will receive an answer.

So why didn't I receive an answer? I did *everything* I was supposed to do! I prayed, I tithed; I went to church every single week. I read the entire Book of Mormon cover to cover . . . I was a good Mormon for years and did what I was supposed to do and never received the testimony that simple investigators are encouraged to find.

. . . I found out recently what I was missing, though. I wasn't asking for mercy. I wasn't asking for God's love to come into my life. I never asked to let God mold me into what he wanted me to be. Honestly, I didn't ask for forgiveness, except to ask forgiveness for not being "good" enough.

Today, I understand what was missing. If all I had were a Catholic church and a priest and the Eucharist, my soul would still leap with joy.

The Eucharist! Oh, my God, how unworthy I am to be in the presence! And yet every time I go into a Catholic church, there he is. In a little over two weeks, I will be able to receive the Blessed Sacrament, our Eucharistic Lord on the altars and in the tabernacles, to have the most intimate communion with God that a person can have on this earth. There is *nothing* in Mormonism like it. Have I mentioned I've been to the temple? Being in the temple doesn't compare to simply sitting in front of the tabernacle in a Catholic church, praying to God and feeling his love wash over me.

So you see, you are wrong about me. The God of Mormonism did not give me an answer to the truth of the Mormon Church because God instead revealed himself to me in the Consecration of the Blessed Sacrament at a Catholic Mass. Through this grace, I have found him as he truly is, Father, Son, and Holy Spirit. I have found him in the heart and soul of the Catholic Church. My joy now is profound.

Mormons Make Great Catholics

I distinctly remember a story heard many times in my youth, told by a leader of the LDS church, LeGrand Richards:

> Many years ago a learned man, a member of the Roman Catholic Church, came to Utah and spoke from the stand of the Salt Lake Tabernacle. I became well acquainted with him, and we conversed freely and frankly. A great scholar, with perhaps a dozen languages at his tongue's end, he seemed to know all about theology, law, literature, science, and philosophy. One day he said to me: "You Mormons are all ignoramuses. You don't even know the strength of your own position. It is so strong that there is only one other tenable in the whole Christian world, and that is the position of the Catholic Church. The issue is between Catholicism and Mormonism. If we are right, you are wrong; if you are right, we are wrong; and that's all there is to it. The Protestants haven't a leg to stand on. For, if we are wrong, they are wrong with us, since they were a part of us and went out from us; while if we are right, they are apostates whom we cut off long ago. If we have the apostolic succession from St. Peter, as we claim, there is no need of Joseph Smith and Mormonism; but if we have not that succession, then such a man as Joseph Smith was necessary, and Mormonism's attitude is the only consistent one. It is either the perpetuation of the Gospel from

> ancient times or the restoration of the Gospel in latter days." (*A Marvelous Work and a Wonder*, 3–4.)

I remember this story as being the reason why people said that Catholics make great Mormons. Since my conversion, I've discovered that Mormons make great Catholics as well. In reflecting on the faith of my childhood compared to the Catholic faith that I now practice, I see many virtues that I held as a Mormon that have carried over to my Catholic faith. One of these virtues is generosity of service, which is one of the fruits of our relationship with Jesus Christ. As a Mormon, I always felt I was most pleasing to God when I fulfilled the callings given to me to serve my church. As a Catholic, I have a much better understanding of the importance of offering the sacrifice of my time and resources in service to others. I fulfill this call to serve God in my faith by volunteering at my parish, and by working for my diocese in the Communications department.

Give Me That Old Time Religion

I love everything about being Catholic, and that includes all of the riches contained in the beautiful history and traditions of Catholicism passed down through the millennia. When I go to a Catholic church, I want it to be as Catholic as possible. I want to see Mary statues and people praying the rosary before Mass, and beautiful stained glass windows. I want lots of candles and incense and pews and altar rails. I want crucifixes and statues of saints and beautiful Stations of the Cross. I want old school confessionals, the kind I always see in movies, with kneelers and a screen between the priest and me. I want priests in cassocks and processions and Eucharistic adoration and all of the rich treasures of my faith. I want to experience the faith of my spiritual fathers in traditions that have been passed down from centuries of saints. I want to know with all five of my senses that I have entered a special place, a holy place set apart to experience and worship God.

While I attend Novus Ordo Masses frequently, I find comfort in the unique style of worship and traditional Catholic devotions I find at my parish, which offers the Mass in what is commonly known as the Extraordinary Form (Latin Masses celebrated in the Roman Rite in accordance with the liturgical books of 1962). I find peace in listening to the Gregorian chant sung by the choir. I loved Gregorian chant long before my conversion and owned quite a few Gregorian chant CDs years before my baptism. I enjoy the feeling of being transported into another world when I see women in chapel veils and hear the bells rung at the Consecration and smell the incense at the High Mass on Sundays. I appreciate the sense of modesty and reverence of the parishioners in the chapel. The priests at this parish are good and holy men, and I have learned much from them on how to grow in holiness and how to truly live my Catholic faith. And, yes, they wear cassocks.

Thankful and Contrite

I thank God every day for the grace to be a daughter of the Church, and for the blessings he gives me to become more fully united to his holy will. I often pray for the conversion of souls and for the sanctification of priests. I spend time with our Eucharistic Lord as often as I can, consoling his most sacred heart in the stillness and darkness of the tabernacle as I kneel before him. I unite my prayers with those of the priest at the altar when he prays in contrition, "*Mea culpa, mea culpa, mea maxima culpa.*"

I offer thanks and praise for the sacrifice Christ made for me at Calvary. I pray in thanksgiving for the love and mercy he freely gives me, unworthy as I am of these gifts. I ask him humbly for the grace to love him as he deserves to be loved, and for a holy death so that I may spend all of eternity praising his holy name and gazing at the radiant beauty of his holy face. And I pray daily for the strength to deny myself, pick up my cross, and follow him.

Cynthia Gill Bates *is the digital media strategist for the Catholic Diocese of Dallas. She served with the USCCB Communications Committee's social media response team in Washington, DC, New York, and Philadelphia during the historic 2015 US Papal Visit. She lives with her husband in Irving, TX, and is a parishioner of Mater Dei Latin Mass Parish.*

The Scuba Diver and the Mermaid

Michael D. Fraley

IN 2000, I WAS sitting in a megachurch with a juice box in my hand, wondering what had gone wrong. The worship service had a back-to-school theme, and the church was trying to shoehorn a communion service into it as well. Thus, the juice box. Even as an Evangelical, I took the Lord's Supper seriously, although I was taught that it was just a symbol. I didn't have the words to describe it then but, if I had, I would have called this sacrilege. The Lord's Supper was a holy thing that had been twisted to fit into someone's Sunday morning program. Good intentions weren't enough. At the time, I went along with it all, hoping that things would take a turn for the better (they didn't), but that was a wake-up call for me, even if the changes I wanted to see in my worship life were slow in coming.

I was raised in a conservative Pentecostal denomination that believed in the moving of the Holy Spirit. People weren't "slain in the Spirit" very often, and I never knew of anyone rolling around on the floor. It was a safe, though not terribly exciting, place, and I came to faith there as a teen. One of my high school teachers was a former Catholic who had come to Christ in a Southern Baptist church. In 1980, he challenged me on my Pentecostal beliefs, and I began to study the history of the moving of the Holy Spirit in the lives of the people of God.

I concluded that if something was true, it was always true in all churches and all historical periods, whether individual people or groups of people believed it or not. With the Lord, I believed that there was "no shadow of turning," just as James 1:17 says. He didn't change his mind. The Lord was stable, his grace and his gifts offered throughout the ebb and flow of history. For the most part, the groups I read about were schismatics like the Waldenses, but my research was still carrying me back in time. A name that resonated with me was Irenaeus, a Christian in the second century, who spoke about the supernatural power of God in his own time. I was intrigued.

Being a constant reader, I eventually found more "missing links" when I ran across a copy of J.B. Lightfoot's *Apostolic Fathers.* More quotes from that Irenaeus fellow followed, but there were also writings from even earlier Christians, such as Ignatius of Antioch and Polycarp of Smyrna. I didn't think of them as "saints" yet, and I certainly didn't think of them as "Catholic," but the picture was beginning to pull together for me.

Over the next several years, I would read much of the work written by the saints who lived before the Council of Nicaea in the fourth century. If nothing else, I realized that they weren't quite like any Christians I had ever known. They believed in baptizing infants and linked their salvation to their baptism. That sounded like heresy to my ears. We only practiced "believer's baptism," just as the early Christians did. Or did they? These were early Christians, some of them instructed by the Apostles. Could everyone everywhere have misinterpreted the Apostles so completely in a matter of just a few decades? That didn't seem likely, especially when I remembered that Christ had promised, "the gates of Hell will not prevail against my Church." (Matt. 16:18). Who was I to call my Lord a liar?

Also, many of these writers had been bishops, or at least priests—unfamiliar words in my world. They loved the Lord's Supper even more than I did, and they seemed to think that there was something supernatural about it. They willingly laid down their lives for this Lord that they loved. Their faith was far from the dead ritual I might have imagined. It was a strong and muscular faith, built to outlast everything thrown against it. Perhaps they were Orthodox, I thought. They certainly lived with a fierce energy and a commitment to the Gospel that was unlike anything Catholic I'd ever encountered.

For many years I found myself in a quandary, enjoying the fellowship of the people in the Evangelical church where I worshiped, but also knowing that I needed something that was beyond my reach, just over the horizon. Then, in 2003, I met the woman who would become my wife. She just happened to be a Catholic.

The real turning point of my faith journey into the Catholic Church came when she took me to Mass. I was stunned. I wept as I heard the Creed, which I had studied for years, professed publicly by the entire congregation. I saw the Eucharist celebrated reverently. I heard the words of the ancient Didache pouring out as the hymn "One Bread, One Body." All of the things that I had spent over twenty years of my life investigating, she had known as part of her everyday world since infancy. I began my RCIA classes that fall and entered the Church at Easter 2004.

For quite a long time, I felt like a scuba diver loaded down with gear, trying to enter the world that my mermaid swam in effortlessly. She was and is devout, but she didn't intellectualize her faith. She had no idea who the early Church Fathers were. She simply believed the teachings of the Church and she lived her faith. I found that to be a beautiful thing.

I realized that I certainly wasn't entering a perfect Church, but I was entering one that God entrusted with the Truth in its most complete, coherent form. I found a church which agreed with the account in Genesis that

God created things that were good, and which used those good and humble elements—water, oil, wheat, and the fruit of the vine—to reach out to us as Sacraments.

I also discovered that the Church was full of heroes, but they sit among the rest of us, on the road to sainthood, and they take us along with them. When I was a teen, I had found Jesus. As an adult, I found myself part of a family; Jesus had also given me a mother in the form of his own mother, Mary. I had come home.

Michael Fraley *is a writer, illustrator, graphic designer, and fine artist who lives with his wife in Fort Wayne, IN.*

Embracing God's Plan for Marriage

Tima Borges

OUR CONVERSION STORY starts ten years into our marriage. While Dave and I were both raised in Catholic families, we had only a vague understanding of what it meant to be Catholic. We attended Mass on most Sundays, prayed occasionally, mostly in times of struggle, and went to Confession once or twice a year during Lent and Advent. We followed the minimum precepts of the Catholic faith.

Our change of heart happened when we learned the Church's teaching on openness to life. When we read St. John Paul II's *Letter to Families* and learned the Theology of the Body, we came to accept God's plan for marriage and family.

We had not always followed the Church's teaching, partly because we did not know God's plan. No one had ever told us, and, if they tried to, we did not fully understand. We thought we had a choice about how to plan our family. Of course, we did—the choice to follow God's plan for marriage and family or to let sin into our marriage.

When we allowed sin into our marriage, our intimacy was hindered. We didn't know why things were going wrong; we just knew something was wrong. Our arguments focused on how often we were intimate and who initiated intercourse. I felt like an object for his pleasure. Spending intimate time with Dave felt like an additional chore to add to my list. Dave could not understand what I was going through. When I tried to communicate with him, he took it personally. As a result, we grew distant and other parts of our marriage were affected. We became simply two adults sharing the same living space. We spoke to each other only when absolutely necessary and then superficially.

Once we positioned ourselves to learn God's plan for marriage and family, our eyes were open. We learned that God designed marriage for the good of man and woman and for the healthy future of society. God created the world and all the creatures in it, but he gave human beings a special dignity, knowledge, intellect, and the natural law. He loves us so much. He shares his creative powers with his creation. Out of our love for each other, we too can create new life in the marital embrace. We perform the physical act and God implants the soul. It's beautiful! How could we not want to be a part of this creation?

We realized God's plan was in line with our human nature, and that it was about love and trust. He always wants the conjugal act to balance unity and openness to life. When we use contraception, we take away our openness to life, which respects our full human nature, all because we want the focus to be solely on unity and enjoyment. The ability to create life is a precious gift, yet we squander it and trample on it for the sake of physical enjoyment.

Looking back, we can see the consequences of our choices, both spiritual and physical. Spiritually we had taken God out of the equation. By using contraception, we were saying to God, "I believe in you, but I don't trust you to know what is best for our family." We paid a hefty price for this choice: struggles in our marriage, unhealthy relationships, and harmful habits that went against our marriage vow and disrespected our dignity as human beings. Not to mention that "the Pill kills," as I now know. How many spontaneous miscarriages did I have in those ten years? Only God knows.

As a result of taking the Pill for ten years, my hormone levels are very low. My uterus probably has aged an extra year for every year that I was on the Pill. My estrogen and progesterone levels are very low. This hormone imbalance also affects my mood and libido.

Dave's vasectomy took something away from our marriage bond; we were incomplete. Thanks to our conversion, he reversed the vasectomy, offering up the risk he took undergoing the surgery and the pain in recovery for all the souls who are yet to come into the light of God's endless mercy and love.

After the vasectomy reversal, we eagerly anticipated welcoming a new baby into our family. We prayed to accept God's will for us, as we had now put this aspect of our marriage in God's hands, where it should have been all along. It took three years and the help of a Napro-technology doctor for us to finally conceive. I have been pregnant three times since then. We have six children, two in Heaven as a result of miscarriages, and four we are blessed to witness growing up.

We recommend further reading and education in this area of God's teaching. Theology of the Body and Saint John Paul II's letters on human dignity and God's plan for marriage and family offer a treasure of information for husbands and wives. There is so much available to us within the Church's two thousand years of experience. It is well worth learning.

Tima Borges *lives with her husband and four boys in Ontario, Canada. She writes for Faith Catholic and shares her powerful testimony of God working in her personal blog. She works with engaged couples preparing for marriage and assists with coordinating faith-based events for women and families.*

Journeys to Peace

Cheryl Ann Wills

I GREW UP IN a Philadelphia suburb. My family was Presbyterian and lived godly values. We were also involved in our church. Every day of any given week, some or all of us were busy in the life of the church. For each of us, this was our choice.

Even so, after high school, I found a gazillion reasons *not* to go to church. The further I moved away from a regular connection to that life, the deeper I sank into the deception of the world. As I heard in a homily once, if you live your faith fast and loose, someone will surely come along and kill it. And by age twenty-eight, I was knocking on death's door with my worldly lifestyle of alcohol and recreational drugs. Being a flower child wasn't about roses. In fact, it led to a dramatic suicide attempt.

My first true realization of God's grace was at that time. Deep inside, I desired *life*—not death. I knew where to turn because of how my parents raised me. I ran back to church, back to Jesus. God's grace renewed me through a charismatic ministry my parents were a part of, called Jesus Focus. I have since made—or at least desire to make—a regular conscious effort to allow God to work through me and to change me, be it ever so slowly, into the image of his Son.

When I was eighteen, I had no intention of marriage before age twenty-five. But out of the blue one day, I told my mother, "I think I'm going to marry a minister." When I met Ed eleven years later, he told me about his call to ministry at age eighteen. He and I are like night and day in so many ways, but our hearts' desire to love and serve the Lord is a common bond that has seen us through every kind of weather. That connection of our hearts is how I immediately knew his call was real and true.

Since Ed was an Episcopalian, I began attending the Episcopal Church. After several years of attending the church of his choice, I came to love the liturgy and its history. The ancient prayers, the secure boundaries of the liturgy in worship spoke to my heart. And I chose to be confirmed in the Episcopal Church, and it became the church of my choice.

A short time after my Confirmation, we moved our family of five from Virginia to Texas. And, though we both loved the liturgy and Sacraments, we joined an independent charismatic church. I loved that little church and its people, but it was there that emptiness and longing began to grow in my heart.

Two years later my husband answered the call that he had heard at age eighteen and was ordained as a

Protestant minister. After Ed's ordination, we moved to northwest New Jersey, which is rural and mountainous. He pastored a nondenominational Protestant congregation as small as the 1908 building in the woods that housed it, white clapboard with a tall steeple.

We lived in this idyllic setting for seven years. While there, we experienced, individually and as a couple, some of our greatest spiritual growth. We truly lived by faith. The church paid for our house and utilities. And Ed's salary of $50 a week covered food, clothing, insurance, and gas—everything for five of us. We never went begging, and we always dressed reasonably well and had our needs met. We didn't mind that we could never afford dinner at a restaurant or a movie at a theater. I remember the first time of many that we sat down to dinner and I whispered to Ed, "This is the last food in the house." We sat down and thanked God for his blessings. And while we ate, we heard a knock at the door. A member of our church stood laden with bags of groceries. It wasn't the only time we witnessed God's mercy providing for us.

But those years of spiritual growth were also the most intense. Despite the indescribable beauty of living in the woods and the miraculous outpouring of God's mercy, most of our growth was like being tested by fire. And much of the growth involved weekly court appearances that culminated in a two-week trial, which ended hands down in our favor.

During that year, Ed and I spent countless hours in prayer together. We walked and prayed. We sat and prayed. We drove and prayed. We prayed first thing in the morning, at midday, and the last thing at night. We became more and more aware of God's presence. We reviewed the day, regardless of how difficult, with gratitude. We paid attention to our emotions and did not let them overtake us. We read and prayed through Scripture. We never lost hope. We continually sought and found God's presence in this extremely hard time of our lives. Satan intended to destroy our marriage and family because he likes best to destroy the foundation of humanity. But Ed and I were discipled through prayer. We grew tremendously closer to each other and to Jesus.

Still, even though my relationship with our Lord grew closer than ever, that strange emptiness and longing expanded. Hateful people who called themselves Christians wore me out, and I felt disillusioned with what I thought to be Christ's church. I very nearly walked away from church—even with a pastor husband.

God uses every twist and turn on our journey to his glory and for our good—*if* we will seek him in those times. He heard my cries, and his grace proved evident once more in my life in 1993. Our little church joined a Protestant denomination, and my husband was ordained an Episcopal priest.

Decades later, God's faithfulness led us into the Catholic Church. Our eyes opened to the reality that

Ed's ordination as a Protestant minister had been only a partial fulfillment of his call. Through the prophetic insight of Pope Benedict XVI, it appears that the way to that fulfillment is through the Personal Ordinariate of the Chair of St. Peter for Anglican clergy, called into existence by this great pope. To support Ed in his call fills me with deep contentment.

This particular Episcopal denomination practiced a liturgical, sacramental, and charismatic style of worship. Inside of me—and even outside—I sang and danced with thanksgiving. Because this new church was founded on the teachings of the Apostolic Fathers, I discovered that what I had considered leaving was what *man* had done to the church, not the church as God established it. That deep emptiness and longing that had begun years earlier began to fill up.

And here began my journey to the Church that Jesus assigned to Peter. By God's grace, my eyes were opened to see what had existed all along. I voraciously read the Church Fathers and other ancient and twentieth century authors. I listened to lectures, in person and on tape, and spent endless hours in discussion with friends who were on the Catholic journey with us.

A few years after finding this denomination, we moved to Kansas City. Once more we were tested as though by fire. To begin with, we felt coerced to move a year before we were comfortable leaving our growing parish in the woods. It was a year before my new home-based business could support us financially. Our oldest daughter was still a missionary, far from home, and we wanted to wait for her return. We tried to convince ourselves and our family and friends that it was important to go. Since the denomination told us to do it, God must surely be in it.

During the first three years, we experienced incredible pain and calamity. My business depended on long-distance communication. In an era of faxes, high phone fees, infant Internet, and no cell phones, it bottomed out. Ed's salary, which we were led to believe was part of the move, did not come to fruition. He could take only a low-paying, part-time job because he needed so much time for his priestly duties. I'll never forget the sinking shock when we looked into our driveway one morning and didn't see our car. It had been repossessed, just four months before it would have been paid off. Friends paid our rent more than once. We had to use food stamps for a few months. Other friends supplied our girls' Christmas gifts for two years.

Because of the emotional pressure of this church with its many unrealistic rules, our oldest daughter, engaged to a fellow missionary, eloped in the middle of their wedding plans. All of us were devastated, especially her sisters who were to be her bridesmaids. One of our daughters had an out-of-body experience in a near-death horse accident. And this mother's heart will always feel pain when I recall the time our daughters, about thirteen and fifteen at the time, said, "Mom, do you think we could buy clothes from a store just once, instead of having only hand-me-downs?" It seemed like every waking moment brought varying levels of sadness, trauma, and uncertainty for our future.

On top of it all, because we now lived closer to the denomination's center of governing politics and their ever-changing rules, we began to see that the people in charge had taken the reins from God. This Protestant denomination—the catalyst for my journey—was no longer consistent with their early teachings. They liked the Catholic look but wanted no part of Catholic authority. Once more, I witnessed the faithfulness of our God as these realities led me to intense study of the Faith and the Catechism.

Eventually, I started skipping church with my family and instead would sit in the back of various Catholic churches during Mass. I wept. And wept. And wept. A gradual awakening began within my head and my heart. Finally, my eyes were opened to how the Holy Spirit has protected and kept pure the deposit of faith given to the early church, regardless of the good or bad people in leadership. Having grown up in denominations that either had a sandy foundation built on protest and rebellion or, worse, made up the rules as they went, I suddenly realized that I longed for stability. A church that preserves its central beliefs for 2000 years is a very solid foundation, a safe place for any believer, a safe place for me.

And then, like a flash of light to a soul agonizing in darkness, I realized that the See of Peter was truly the authority given by God to govern his Church. My soul burst with joy that I could not contain! And this life-changing revelation made my future path clear: if I honestly desired the fullness of my faith, then I had to submit to the authority of the Catholic Church.

But how could I go alone? I had a family. Another example of his grace in our midst: God brought my husband, our younger daughters who still lived at home, and myself, individually, to the same desire. By Easter of 2000, we had all entered the Church.

A sigh of relief? Not quite. In fact, our conversion caused others pain. The people in the old church were ninety-nine percent of our friend base, since we had lived in the Midwest only a short time. They abandoned us. Hateful things were said about us. Our daughters ached that their youth leaders, whom they had confided in, and all the kids in the youth group were instructed not to contact them. God's faithful grace abounds. I give him thanks for the healing salve of forgiveness. It healed my wounds and set me free. And because of his gift of forgiveness, I am fully reconciled to all who were involved.

There are only two decisions I've made in my life that I can say this about: the peace that I knew in my heart at the point of each of those conscious decisions has continued to grow deeper the further I am from that point. Those two decisions were to marry my wonderful husband and to submit to the authority of the Catholic Church. It is the peace that passes all understanding.

Nothing is more important in all of life than our relationship with God, through his only Son. I firmly believe there is nothing we should put more energy into than that relationship. For this reason, as a relatively new convert to the Church, I would give this admonition to people who are young in the faith:

Learn your faith inside and out. Guard and protect your faith. Commit to living it fully. If you "live your faith fast and loose," you *will* meet those who will attempt to kill it. You may even kill it yourself. Your place in the Church is unique and planned. Continually seek the plan that God has for you here. Some in the Church are converts, like me. Some were baptized into the faith in infancy. For each of us, this church is an inestimable gift. For 2000 years, God's children have been given the privilege of taking refuge in the wounds of Jesus in his Church. Let that refuge be your peace. His children are honored to receive his grace to carry on, beginning with their baptism and continuing through the Body and Blood of his only begotten Son. As the deep knowledge of that honor permeates your soul, and as you participate in the Sacraments, you will be changed into the image of his Son.

When I receive our Lord in the Eucharist, I shed tears of gratefulness that he brought me to this place, and for his Real Presence. They are also tears accompanied by an internal shudder when I think of how close I was to missing the gift of the Catholic Church.

How did I almost miss it? I was busy striving to *build* the church, a sadly misguided Protestant notion. The reality is that the Church *is* built and the blood of the martyrs has paved the way for her work. They have paved the way for us to *be* the Church—to be the hands and feet of Jesus on the earth. We, the Church, feed the hungry, clothe the poor, shelter the homeless, visit the prisoner, care for the widow and the orphan. And through the Sacraments, we know the power of his grace to work in and through us to those ends.

Has life been sugar sweet and easy since we entered the Church? Absolutely not. But because of the life, death, and resurrection of Jesus, the blood of the martyrs, the work of the Holy Spirit, and the gift of the Sacraments, my spiritual journey will continue in that safe place which God has made for his children, the one Holy Catholic and Apostolic Church. And my life on earth can face every trial with strength and confidence.

I am home, at last, with my fellow sisters and brothers in Christ. My heart rejoices—moment by moment.

Cheryl Ann Wills *is an author and entrepreneur. She writes non-fiction, children's stories, and inspirational works such as* Who is Jesus? First Century Eyewitnesses Tell Their Stories. *You can visit her at CherylAnnWills.com. Cheryl and her husband Ed live in Kansas City, MO.*

Finding Jesus in My Life

John Chomistek

I'VE HAD FLEETING times and moments of contemplating if there is a God. Was there really this Jesus Man-God that walked the earth some two thousand years ago? I have always been able, though, to see those moments of uncertainty as just a passing thought and again concluded that God and Jesus were in fact real.

Sometimes it has taken hard lessons to regain my faith in Jesus. For example, in the winter of my sophomore year at college, I stopped going to church. It was scary. Those three months turned out to be the worst, loneliest, and darkest time in my life, as the glitter of the world displaced God. It was not until I rediscovered the gift of the Mass that spring that joy again replaced the darkness.

But it took a life-changing event twenty years ago to truly cement my belief in Jesus as my God and Savior. It is true that God has a purpose and a reason for everyone. I didn't know what that purpose was or even that God had a purpose in mind for me until I was forty years old.

I will never forget the year 1996. It was the year that God visited me personally, and I was not the same afterward.

In the '50s and '60s, Archbishop Fulton Sheen had an Emmy award-winning TV show on which he evangelized Americans to spread Jesus' Good News. In one show, he talked about the Magi's visit to the Holy Family that first Christmas. He said, "Of course, the Magi took another route home. When one encounters Jesus, one can never go back the same way one came."

In 1996 I was involved with the Christ Renews His Parish (CHRP) program at my parish in Indianapolis, the same program we have at my current parish in Texas, Our Lady of Angels. I was in my formation period after my first retreat, working with my fellow CRHP brothers preparing the next retreat. We had homework to study between each weekly meeting. One evening, while engrossed in my studies, I felt the presence of the Holy Spirit. I suddenly had to stop what I was doing to address this feeling.

The call was similar to God's calling of the Old Testament Prophet Samuel from his deep sleep in 1 Samuel:3. I said, "Yes, Lord, I am listening." In this first encounter, I received one sole message: that God loved me.

In the weeks to follow, the phenomenon happened again. I would feel the presence of the Holy Spirit. I would stop what I was studying and listen. These next four weeks, though, I received a very different message. This message stated, "Something very bad will happen to you and your family." The end of each message always contained a flowing, total peace that I seemed just to inhale. Peace that I had never received or felt before.

In later visitations, I began to ask, "What will this bad thing be? Will someone from my family be hurt or lost?"

Jesus answered this question with, "No, all will be safe and unhurt."

How great it was not only to hear God speaking to me but actually hold a conversation with him! Doubts, though, raged through my mind. Was this real? Was I just making this up? Was this really coming from God and not from some other spirit trying to bring harm to me?

The key evidence that this was coming from God was that total feeling of peace. I knew I could not make up something like that. I knew that the Devil could not produce peace, only anger and confusion. Secondly, I probably received at least ten different visitations, so this was more than just a passing thought or daydream.

About four months after these visitations finally ended, and just as God had predicted, the bad thing happened. Early in the morning of July 5, 1996, our home caught fire and burned down. We lost everything we owned.

The Miracle

First, the miracle: God promised that we would all make it out safely. All the elaborate pieces God put together, the sequence of events to make all this happen, were amazing.

First, our family had gone on a cookout the day before, on the Fourth of July. The barbecued food had given my wife heartburn, so that she slept restlessly that night. About two o'clock in the morning my oldest son, then nine years old, woke up to use the bathroom, something that he had never done before. His clattering around in the bathroom woke up my lightly sleeping wife. She then smelled a faint burning odor and woke me up.

I walked through the house hoping to confirm that all was okay so could we could go back to bed. But when I checked the garage, the ceiling was all bright orange, on fire. I ran upstairs, woke up my wife and three children, and we all left the house, completely unhurt. No one saw even a single flame on the way out, completing God's promise to me: everyone was okay.

After the firemen came, I was standing with the fire captain watching the firefight when it finally hit me like a two-by-four to the back of the head: this was it! This was the bad thing foretold. First, I realized that the fire was the final piece to prove those visits earlier in the year were in fact from God. The thing foretold had happened, just as predicted in those visitations.

After that, my knees became weak. I felt like Moses witnessing the burning bush, except that my house was definitely being consumed. I felt as if I were standing on holy ground, on a holy quest. I knew then that losing all my possessions in this fire was one part of God's plan.

He had done so much to prepare me for this. I knew that there had to be more.

That "something more" began to happen the next morning. People started coming out of the woodwork to donate things to my family that we had lost and needed: clothes, shoes, toys for the children, sheets, towels. Our neighbors took us in and housed and fed us. Our parish took up a second collection for us at all the Masses the next weekend.

God's plan? Through my family and me, through our house fire, the Holy Spirit was sent to energize the love of our communities surrounding my family.

The most awesome gift I received was seeing Jesus in each person who came to generously fill our needs. I saw their eyes light up. Their faces seemed to get brighter with each step taken from their car to the house where we stayed. We had always heard in our religious education classes that Jesus resides in each of us. Well, I am telling you it is true. I saw it!

I tell you, God is real! Jesus is real! I do not have to expound some grand quest of science to prove that God is real. He is real. I interacted with him. He loves me. He told me that. The bad thing he predicted really happened. My family was completely unhurt just as he promised. I saw Jesus in each person who visited us during that year to give us support. I watched Jesus explode out from their eyes. They looked like angels. I have never questioned the reality of God again. How could I?

The best thing is that, of all the billions of people on this earth, God knew me. He knew all about me. He knew how weak I was. He knew I would need to be strengthened to bear his Cross to energize my community.

Even better, Jesus knows each one of you. He loves each one of you infinitely. He wants all of us to be with him for all eternity. All we need to do is say, "Yes." It doesn't get any better than that! Amen.

***John Chomistek** wrote a book about his experience,* I Have Come to Set the Earth on Fire. *At Our Lady of Angels parish in Allen, TX, he serves as an Extraordinary Minister of the Holy Communion and a high school catechist, as well as in the Knights of Columbus, Boy Scouts, RCIA, Christ Renews His Parish, Right to Life, and That Man Is You. He blogs at House on Fire Publications.*

Fireman, Doctor, or Priest?

Bishop Mark J. Seitz

Do you remember summer days as a kid when you were free? Free just to be outside, feeling the summer sun warming your face even as a gentle breeze cooled it? There was no job to do, no appointment to keep. You had time just to be and to take note of textures and colors, crisp blue skies, a rich carpet of green grass punctuated by dazzling rows of flowers. You had time to reflect and to dream. I can recall a time like this, a long time ago when I was eight years old. The cherished memory has been protected by me all these fifty years and counting, because I made a firm commitment always to remember that moment.

It is not that anything earthshaking took place at that moment. In many ways, it was a very ordinary event. God did not open the heavens and speak to me. No miraculous occurrence unfolded before me. I was just standing in front of the garage at my family's home in Hartland, Wisconsin, enjoying a moment of quiet reflection in the warm summer sun. If the moment was at all extraordinary, I suppose, it would have to do with the fact that at that moment, I was alone. By that time I already had five of what eventually became nine brothers and sisters. The solitary moments were limited.

As I stood there in that graced moment, I began to think adventurously about what I would like to do with my life. Three options came quickly to the surface. I would like to be a fireman, a doctor, or—a priest. All three possibilities excited me. Each of them held great challenge and struck me as very fulfilling ways to spend my life. For a moment, with the exuberance of youth, I considered whether I might possibly be able to become all three. I could be "Mark Seitz, Fireman-Doctor-Priest." Wouldn't that be great! I could provide all the services necessary when a person was in great need. I could rescue them from a burning building, resuscitate them, and, if that did not work, offer last rites.

My parents and grandparents had always told me I could be anything I really wanted to be. They had always affirmed that I would be able to do great things with my life. God had a wonderful and exciting plan for me, and nothing that God wanted for me would be impossible. I count this as among the greatest gifts my family gave to me. They taught me to dream ambitious dreams. But they also gave me the conviction that my fulfillment in life would come not from any monetary or material accumulation. I would find fulfillment insofar as my life made a difference for others. I wanted to make a difference.

Fireman. Doctor. Priest. Those three possibilities all seemed very attractive but, even at my tender age, I realized that the day might come when I would have to make a choice among these options. After all, I did not want to be in school for my whole life!

So, as I continued to stand peacefully with a gentle breeze stroking my face, I reasoned further. If I were a fireman, I could pull people from burning buildings and save their lives. That would be a wonderful thing. If I were a doctor, I could heal those who were sick. That would be a great way to live my life. It occurred to me, though, that, despite my best efforts, eventually those people would die. No one on this earth lives forever. But if I were a priest, my eight-year-old brain reasoned, I could not only help them in this life; I could save them forever!

So the decision was kind of simple. If I had to choose between being a fireman, a doctor, or a priest, I would like to be a priest. What a great way that would be to spend my life. I wanted to be a priest! I knew it would be a long time before that would become a reality. Maybe I would end up deciding on something else. But if I became a priest, I would remember that, when I was eight years old and standing in the summer sun in front of our house at 212 Circle Drive in Hartland, Wisconsin, I decided what I wanted to be.

There is much more to the story since that day. Long periods of time went by when I gave no thought to the conclusion I had come to in the summer sun. Many times passed when I was not at all sure what my calling really was. I had to discern whether my desire to be a priest came from God or from myself. Ultimately, my vocation depended not on my choosing but upon God's plan for my life. That moment of insight when I was eight helped spur years of prayer and discernment. With the help of God and of many people, I continued to progress. Eventually, through eight years of reflection and growth in the seminary, God's call to me became clear.

When I first entered the seminary as a freshman in college, I was in seventh heaven. I doubt that I had ever been so happy. My final years of high school had been good years. In some ways, I had come into my own and I had a great group of friends, but the question of what I wanted to do with my life weighed upon me.

The day I entered the seminary, the questions and doubts about what my next step should be fell away. Here was a place I didn't know existed in this life. I encountered a group of young men like myself, who valued what I valued and sought what I sought. Those who led the seminary were tough. They made it clear that we had to toe the line or we would be out. I appreciated that and what I appreciated even more was that they were men of the Church into whose hands I could entrust my formation.

My studies at the University of Dallas where all the seminarians attended classes were also a source of satisfaction. I had never studied so hard, but the Faith imbued everything we learned. I was like a sponge soaking it all up. More than once, fellow seminarians came up to me and said, “Seitz, why are you always smiling?” I was surprised by the question because I hadn’t noticed. But upon further reflection, I realized that it was just because I was so happy to be there.

That being said, I cannot say that every day was a happy day. Discernment of a vocation, if it is good discernment, should challenge a person and their unexamined conclusions to the core and, during my eight years of seminary, this was frequently the case for me.

I particularly remember a time when I was in my second year at Holy Trinity. We were having a day of recollection, a one-day retreat on a Sunday. A fellow seminarian brought a message to me: “The Rector wants to see you this afternoon at three o’clock.” Fear struck my heart! When the Rector called one in, it was not so he could pat you on the back and tell you that you were a model seminarian. When a person was called in outside the normal course of things, it could well be to tell you to pack your bags and go home.

I spent that day in one of the most intense examinations of conscience I had ever done. I considered what I might have done or failed to do. I felt very contrite even though I didn’t know what I should feel sorry for.

By the time I entered the Rector’s office, I was a wreck. My knees were knocking. The Rector informed me that he was suspicious of me because I seemed to be too compliant. He assured me he would be watching. That was a tough day!

Another day comes to mind; I believe it was during my junior year of college, when the academics were wearing me down and things just seemed hard at the seminary. I remember walking up a wooded hill near the seminary and wrestling with these questions. I asked myself, what I might choose to do if I left the seminary? I remembered that the priesthood was one of the several exciting options from my childhood. I had thought I would also like to be a fireman or a doctor. The role of fireman no longer held an attraction, but I could still imagine myself being a physician.

Nevertheless, even in the midst of that difficult moment when the peace and joy had left me, when I considered that option alongside a call to the priesthood it was no match. As hard as it was, in the midst of all the questioning and doubts, I could only see myself being happy and fulfilled in the priesthood.

The words of St. Peter to Jesus, spoken at the conclusion of Chapter 6 in the Gospel of John, hit me like a bolt of lightning. Many of those who had listened to Jesus speaking of himself as the Bread of Life had found his teaching too hard to accept. As they were departing, Jesus turned to the Twelve and asked, “And you, will you leave me too?” Peter spoke the words that were on my heart in that low moment, “Lord, to whom shall we go? You have the words of eternal life.”

By that time, I had come to know that what had been stirring in my heart all these years was not simply a matter of finding what I wanted, it was a matter of discovering a dream that God had held for me from the moment he created me. My vocation in life—what would truly bring me peace, joy, and fulfillment, as well as a cross—was only my response in harmony with God's good plan. He planted the seed in my heart in the only way I could grasp it as a young child. Patiently, God waited through many events of my life, both joyful and difficult ones, before I could even grasp the right question to ask. Then he led me through the darkness step by faltering step. At each step of the way the questions arose, many new challenges came, but, even in the darkest moments of doubt, the answer of Peter sustained me and I continued the journey.

I cannot say I ever knew without a doubt that he was calling me until, after many small steps, one day the Church, through the bishop, called me to Holy Orders. What a great reassurance to know that it was not only me discerning—it was the Church as well, through the seminary staff and the bishop!

A beautiful day that I will always remember is May 17, 1980. At my home parish in Okauchee, Wisconsin, Bishop Thomas Tschoepe, the Bishop of Dallas, laid hands on my head and ordained me to the Priesthood of Jesus Christ for the Diocese of Dallas. That day I was sure the calling was from God. Thanks be to God, although many challenges and many difficult days are mingled among the many, many joyful and fulfilling ones, I have never ever doubted God's call. I am a priest! I belong to him!

To this day, I still think it would have been neat to be a fireman or a doctor. Still, I would never trade the joy and the fulfillment I have experienced as a priest. Yes, I had to choose one great vocation and leave some others behind. But I have to tell you a little secret: as a priest, and now, since 2010, a bishop, I have been called on many occasions to assist families who have lost everything to fire. Innumerable times I have been privileged to walk the halls of hospitals bringing Christ's comfort and the wonderful spiritual medicine of the Anointing of the Sick. In many ways, my original dream has been realized. I have indeed become a fireman, a doctor—and a priest.

***Bishop Mark J. Seitz**, a native of Wisconsin, studied, was ordained, and served in the Diocese of Dallas for more than forty years before becoming Bishop of the Diocese of El Paso in 2013. His motto is* Paratum cor meum—*"My heart is ready."*

Sharing Your Galilee Moment

Gloria Castro

"He said to them, 'Go into the whole world and proclaim the Gospel to every creature.'" (Mark 16:15)

WE ARE CALLED to share our testimony with others in our daily walk. Some of us have been called to tell our story at the ACTS retreat in thirty minutes, but I am not referring to those testimonies. I am referring to a five-minute encounter with a coworker, family member, neighbor, or someone you meet in your daily walk. As you grow in the Lord and experience changes in your life, people will notice. They may ask, "What it is that gives you that assurance that things are going to get better?" Or someone may say, "I would be so troubled if this or that happened in my life, but you seem to be at peace." Times like this are ideal for sharing your faith story.

My faith journey began when I was a child. Our parents always made sure we went to church and Sunday School. I would now describe what happened when I was eighteen as a Galilee moment—that moment when

I first met Jesus, as the Apostles did in Galilee. My neighbor, a Baptist minister, had me read the Sinner's Prayer. The moment I prayed it, I felt something that I can hardly describe. Whatever it was, it gave me a hunger and thirst for what I felt at that moment. The only thing I can compare it to is when I hear of people experiencing cocaine for the first time. It is so amazing that they want to experience that same feeling of wholeness again and again, so they keep sniffing it to get that first experience again.

I have never forgotten the encounter I had with Christ that day. It was as if I had been told all my life about the Lord, but this day I knew I had experienced something so amazing and wonderful. He didn't ask me to start going to church and stop living the way I was living. He just showed me unconditional love by giving me an assurance of peace that I had never felt before.

Life has a lot of ups and downs and distractions. So many times, we sense the Lord directing us as he did the disciples, to return to where we first responded to his call, to that Galilee moment when we first met Jesus and knew that he loves us.

Many times we can walk so strongly with the Lord and then find ourselves getting distracted with everyday issues. We realize that something is missing—the excitement of being in the Word is no longer there, our faith has dwindled, and problems are occurring. Then something will happen, and again we will remember that

Galilee moment. My experience of returning to my Galilee moment relates to the story of the Samaritan woman:

> The woman left her water jar and went into the town and said to the people, "Come see a man who told me everything I have done. Could he possibly be the Messiah?" (John 4:28–29)

I couldn't get over my past, the sin that I remembered often. Then a woman I didn't know told me that the Lord wanted me to quit looking at the curtain behind me because there was nothing there. At first, I didn't know what she meant. I asked the Lord to show me if this was from him, so I could receive it as from him. If not, then I asked him to help me forget about it.

The following Sunday during Mass I began to cry, because the understanding of what she had said came over me like a flash. The Lord sent this woman to tell me to quit looking back at the curtain so that I would know he had forgiven me in my Galilee moment.

This kind of personal sharing brings hope to others that can't seem to let go of things concerning their past. It will draw them to want to experience a life filled with trust in the Lord in small and big areas of their lives.

Gloria Castro *is a retired broadcasting software operator, ready to witness the love of God wherever she goes. God has blessed her and her husband Amado with two children and two grandchildren. She is on the ACTS Ministry leadership team and serves as an Extraordinary Minister of Holy Communion and a lector. Her passion is witnessing to the love of God and praying with and for others.*

A Jewish Physicist's Conversion Story

Robert Kurland

I GREW UP AS a secular Jew, despite having several rabbis as great-grandparents. In the great wisdom of early adolescence, I refused to be Bar-Mitzvahed, believing it to be a sham ceremony in a world with so much misery and injustice—misery and injustice ignored by those fur-coated ladies parading in Temple.

Nevertheless, I had a belief of sorts in a Creator. My teenage passion was astronomy. Visiting the local planetarium and constructing (not well) a six-inch reflecting telescope made me mindful of the truth expressed in Psalm 19: "The heavens declare the glory of God." One summer when I worked in the Yosemite forest service, I remember lying beneath one of the big trees, filled with awe at the Creator's work here on earth.

My wife is Catholic, and we married in the Catholic Church, but I kept my distance from the Church, attending only baptisms and functions at my children's Catholic school. At one of these, my oldest daughter's baptism, I was embarrassed to be asked to serve as an altar server for the priest. My protestations that I wasn't Catholic were of no avail.

Now, into each life some rain must fall, and fall it did in mine. Without going into detail and violating confidences, I'll say that in my 60s I became a member of a Twelve Step group: "Hi, I'm Bob, and I'm a (fill in the blank)." A guiding principle of such groups is the presence of a Higher Power (uppercase obligatory), who will help to break addictive chains (alcohol, drugs, food, persons). I was disposed to believe in the presence of such a Higher Power, but I came to realize that the phrase was doublespeak, Orwellian "sheer cloudy vagueness," a euphemism for God. I began to search for a more satisfying way to think about the deity (at that time in lowercase).

Fortunately, at this point the Holy Spirit intervened, prompting me to read *Who Moved the Stone?* by Frank Morison, a pseudonym for Albert Henry Ross. Ross was a British writer who originally set out to disprove the Resurrection, but who, on evaluating the Biblical accounts, came to believe. I won't recount the evidence found in the articles on my website, but it seemed to me that an impartial jury (not composed of evangelical atheists) considering the evidence that the Resurrection was "made up" would give a verdict of "not guilty"—i.e., the arguments that the Biblical accounts of the Resurrection were true.

What struck me, even more, moving from *Who Moved the Stone?* to the New Testament, was that this bunch of uneducated yahoos—fishermen, tax collectors, women—had managed to out-talk the scholars of Judaism and thereby to spread the Christian faith through the Roman world. Surely they must have been inspired by encounters with the risen Jesus and the inner voice of the Holy Spirit.

It also occurred to me that, if one does believe in the Gospel account of the Resurrection, then one should also believe other incidents described there, in particular, the words of Jesus giving the keys of the Kingdom to Peter, thus founding the Catholic Church. Accordingly, the Christian religion to which I would convert should be Roman Catholic. This choice also eliminated a certain amount of domestic controversy.

I must emphasize that this whole process was one of rational decision-making—no visions, no voices—whence "Top Down to Jesus." I envy those who have had visions of our Lord and heard his voice. I have heard firsthand accounts of such from some of my friends, but this was not my good fortune.

Of course, conversion is an ongoing process—study, service, prayer, adoration, retreats, all the tools and fertilizer to make the fig tree of faith bear ever more fruit. To recount this continuing process fully would take a chapter, not a short essay, but I'll add these brief comments.

First, as a scientist, I struggled to believe in miracles. Fr. Mc's answer to questions on certain dogmas during my catechesis helped: "If you believe in one miracle, the Resurrection, why are you having problems with others?" and "If you believe in the possibility, even if you have questions, that is enough." As I looked at the evidence for contemporary miracles, particularly that reported by Dr. Alexis Carrell at Lourdes, and read what C. S. Lewis and Ralph McInerny had to say about the reality of miracles, my scientific skepticism waned.

Second, those few non-"Top Down" but "In the Heart" moments when I felt the presence of the Deity (although not well defined, not as an image or as a voice) have been evoked by music: Gregorian chant during a retreat at St. Vincent Archabbey, certain hymns and liturgical music, and (very, very infrequently) at quiet times in the early morning during adoration or other prayer, when the melody of some favorite hymn would come to mind.

Now, I claim that this belief in Jesus and the doctrine of the Catholic Church, this faith, is, in certain respects, akin to and also different from my belief (faith) in science. To begin with, let me assert that by no means can science explain everything; that is to say, "scientism" is a false doctrine.

The books of Keith Ward, the writings of Fr. Stanley Jaki (particularly *The Limits of a Limitless Science*), and most recently an essay by the eminent biologist Austin

Hughes on "The Folly of Scientism" effectively demolish the positions of evangelical atheists such as Dawkins, Hawking, Kraus, and Carroll, who believe that science is the only answer. They ignore all that science can't explain, the "why" questions. For example, they believe that since we can show by functional MRI where the brain is active when we pray or contemplate, we fully understand how and what the mind is doing in prayer or mystical experience. Wrong!

Most people put the same faith in what science tells them as the Christian faithful do in the dogmas of the Church. How many people have done Galileo's inclined-plane experiment to verify laws of motion, as I did in the physics lab at Caltech, and so forth? The essence of the scientific method is that theoretical predictions can be verified by repeated measurements, and this, in turn, implies that those things and realities that cannot be quantified and realized by an experiment or measurement cannot be dealt with scientifically. And, even then, science is limited to setting up idealized experiments, situations isolated from surroundings in which the hypothesized experiment may not always be possible.

In desperation to avoid the act of creation that implies the Deity, theoretical physicists are putting their faith in multiverse theories—"M-theories" with infinite landscapes. These theories are most unlikely to be verified experimentally (i.e., capable of being falsified), exercises in mathematical metaphysics even more removed from one's experience than that supposedly posited by Medieval theologians regarding how many angels could stand on the point of a pin. (This is actually a reasonable question: "How many immaterial entities can be contained in a point?")

Indeed, it is clear that there are questions that cannot readily be framed in the lucid framework of physical science. These include the butterfly wings beating in China that produce the tornado in Oklahoma; the organization of life, springing from disorder, as shown by the Nobel prize winner Ilya Prigogine; mathematical unknowability, which is surprising and possibly not in everyone's everyday experience.

To sum up, let me assert that religious faith can be attained by a variety of roads—by a vision, by a voice from above, or by rational "Top Down" endeavor. To paraphrase Shakespeare's *Twelfth Night*, "some are born with faith, some achieve faith, and some have faith thrust upon them." And the faith we have in Jesus Christ is as well founded, in terms of empirical evidence and inner knowledge, as the faith we physicists have in what science tells us about the world.

***Robert Kurland**—convert, blogger, teacher, musician—describes himself as a "cranky, old retired physicist trying to show that there is no contradiction between what science tells us about the world and our Catholic faith." He serves as an Extraordinary Minister of Holy Communion and lector, and volunteers at a federal prison and hospital.*

What is Truth?

Jeannie Ewing

AS A CRADLE Catholic, I never questioned my faith or strayed too far from it during the formative years. I recall spending lots of time when I was a small child lingering in my bedroom, lost in my thoughts about God, Heaven, the angels, and saints. I often prayed, as it came naturally to me to speak with God as a friend. I also knew the angels and saints were real and could assist me in times of need.

Of course, adolescence sparked skepticism and disillusionment with the Catholic Church for a short time. I no longer attended Catholic school. Every variety of socioeconomic status, race, ethnicity, and religion filled my huge metropolitan high school. One of the boys whose locker was across from mine was an open Satanist. For the first time in my life, I questioned what I believed.

This questioning was mostly because I formed friendships with zealous Protestants who attended Pentecostal and other Evangelical denominations. I firmly stood my ground on the Trinity and knew Jesus was my Savior, but some of the rites and rituals of Catholicism no longer made sense to me. Unfortunately, though I had received an eight-year Catholic education, I wasn't well catechized and didn't know how to defend my faith.

As I entered my sophomore year, I approached my parents to inquire about attending other Protestant churches with some of my friends. Many of them were active in their youth groups, and I wanted to be a part of that. I had always longed for God—pined for him, even—but I was temporarily confused about where my church home should be.

I didn't know it at the time, but my parents were deeply troubled at my desire to "church shop." They prayed about it and discussed it among their close-knit group of friends from our parish (and even our pastor). Then they reluctantly agreed that I could attend Protestant youth group and services—*as long as* I still went to weekly Mass with them.

The deal was sufficient for me, and off I went—to Baptist, Lutheran, Assembly of God, and nondenominational megachurches, among others. At first, I basked in the feel-good aspect of their worship style. I loved the live bands and extravagant, dynamic preaching. The only thing that bothered me about most of these modern churches was that there was no real altar anywhere. It looked more like a stage to me—and without a cross or crucifix.

All along, I prayed that God would lead me to truth. The question of Pilate burned in my heart every day: "What is truth?" I wrestled with it, unaware that my parents and Catholic church family were fervently praying for me to find my way back home. After a few months of the pomp and circumstance at these huge Protestant churches, I didn't feel comfortable there anymore.

I was frustrated that there was no real liturgy. I found comfort in the rituals of the Mass, even if I didn't understand them. I was also bothered that everyone kept asking me if I was "saved" once they discovered I was Catholic. I had to ask myself if I was saved and what that meant. But the defining moment that brought me back to the Catholic faith—when I authentically claimed it as *my* faith—happened during a "communion" service at one nondenominational megachurch.

I had attended Mass that Sunday morning, according to the agreement with my parents, but I decided to tag along to the evening worship service with some of my friends from school at this well-known local congregation. After the usual praise and worship opening, the bishop (whose role I really couldn't discern clearly) played up the fact that this particular weekend was so special because it was their monthly communion service.

Taken aback that they didn't partake in communion weekly, I waited with bated breath for what was to come next. Aghast, I saw ushers walk up the aisles with silver trays filled with tiny cups of what appeared to be grape juice, along with bite-sized pieces of sandwich bread.

Really?!

I was disgusted, yet perplexed at the same time. What was this all about, and why did it bother me? When it came time for our row to partake of this odd symbolic ritual, I politely declined. The usher insisted, but I stood my ground of refusal. After that evening, I never went back to that church.

The following Sunday, I prayed in desperation to the Lord, asking him why that instance was so insulting in my mind. Up until that moment, I was fairly certain I wasn't going to claim Catholicism as my faith of choice. Little did I realize that this interior struggle occurred during the Consecration. I was kneeling during this intense silent prayer, and all at once—just like in the movies—I slowly raised my head as our pastor elevated the Host and finalized the prayers of Consecration.

In that instant, I knew. I knew what those churches were missing and why I was so offended at their weak gesture of communion. It was this—the Eucharist—Jesus' true Body, Blood, Soul, and Divinity—that had been missing all along. At that moment, I felt as if I had found some lost treasure, and all at once, I knew that Catholicism was my true home.

Receiving Jesus shortly thereafter solidified everything I had questioned. I became a zealous Catholic, hungrily devouring everything I could learn in order to understand

and defend the tenets of the Faith. I joined our youth group and, eventually, young adult ministry. After high school, I began attending daily Mass with my mom, as well as adoration and praying a daily rosary and Divine Mercy chaplet.

Those early young adult years were the springtime of my life and my faith. I cannot say that, since that time, my faith has never been tested. During the many trials that have tested my faith, I knew that fidelity to God and his Church would keep me from being led astray.

Somehow, even in the midst of those mysteries that have no answer this side of Heaven, I have learned that the most valuable treasure I do have is the Faith my parents gave me and that I continue to claim as my own.

Not everything in life has a smooth and easy answer. In fact, I believe that most trials are meant to indicate whether our faith is genuine, but that refinement of virtue is what keeps us following Jesus and knowing that we have at our disposal the key to unlocking the truth we seek. I am grateful to say that I found my answer to "What is truth?" The truth is in Catholicism, a beautiful and priceless gift for us all.

Jeannie Ewing, *a Catholic spirituality writer, has published* From Grief to Grace *and* Waiting with Purpose, *as well as a meditation journal and a devotional. She is a frequent guest on Catholic radio and contributes to several online and print Catholic periodicals. Her website is jeannieewing.com.*

This Journey of a Lifetime

Elizabeth Reardon

MY FRESHMAN YEAR at Mount Holyoke College was an exciting time of rigorous study, new friendships, challenging adjustments, and unbelievable growth. Over twelve hundred miles away from home, I found myself seeking both comfort in the familiar but also joy in discovering who I was to become. Though I studied hard and partied equally so, I still made time to attend church either on campus or locally in town with a classmate. I noticed that something was missing, something I couldn't define, but leaving me incomplete. Perhaps the experience of worship had changed or I had—or even a bit of both.

Then one Sunday, as the minister spoke metaphorically of finding one's center, I suddenly realized that something *was* missing. What I longed for was not a vague pulpit description of what God is, but a concrete awareness of who God is *in my life*. And while I knew my center was Christ, I no longer felt his presence as near and tangible. My soul yearned for so much more.

Intense and undeniable, I truly felt God working within me over the course of the proceeding months, asking me to let go and let him lead.

It wasn't until a late night out had caused me to miss the first half of the Protestant service that my desire to be with God and my searching all came together.

I could go back to my dorm room, I thought. But wait, a Catholic Mass was starting soon. Rather than arrive uncomfortably late, I could be on time. I knew so little of Catholic practices. Would my unfamiliarity be too easily distinguishable? What I heard in response within my heart was: "This is an opportunity to find what you have been searching for. God is here."

I turned the handle on the door of the chapel and took my seat near the middle of the church. I knelt before God for the first time. In this silence before Mass began, I found such peace and comfort in my anonymity. Here in this sacred time and place, I whispered, "I am here too, Father." Admittedly, as Mass began and I looked to my left and right for guidance, it was all too obvious that I was a newcomer. Just when I started questioning the reasoning that had brought me here, God reached out and drew me close. Those on either side stretched out their hands as the beautiful, familiar words of the Our Father echoed throughout the chapel space. I was home.

Soon after that, I was to discover the love of my life in a deep friendship that had begun earlier that fall with a Catholic sophomore at UMass Amherst. When I look back, it seems every detail of our meeting and courtship was just as it was intended to be. Neither of us was initially looking for a long-term relationship, but we each were honestly seeking someone who reflected the values we held dear. Reluctantly, he accepted that I was not ready to date but longed for his friendship. Through months of listening to one another tell of the faults of those we dated, and giving advice, we grew closer. John was waiting for me and loving me all the while. I couldn't believe how blessed I was that God had planned it all! Though we frequently attended Mass together, for some time I still held back in telling him how God was moving me ever closer to conversion. With prayer and discernment so significant in my life, I was cautious and wanted to be certain that this was indeed where God was leading me to go.

When that moment arrived, there was no looking back, and I knew the time had come to speak to Fr. Infantini and my family about my decision to enter RCIA. With a knock on the door, and a commitment to pursue God's calling, my searching heart was filled with a fullness of faith, joy, and love. And, to my surprise, my family not only respected my faith decision but prayed and supported me throughout it all. To this day, I still remember the phone call to my mother. After sharing the events that had brought me to this place, there was a long pause for what seemed like an eternity.

"It all makes sense now," was her response.

"What makes sense?" I curiously asked.

"Before you were born, I had a dream that you would be a Catholic. Standing before a multitude of others gathered, you then spoke passionately of your love and faith in God. I know now that God was preparing me for this day."

"Mom, why have you never told me this before?"

"Well, I didn't want to persuade you, should that not be God's will. I knew that, if it was, God would certainly lead you there."

As I hung up the phone, I felt awe at God's magnificence and confirmation that I was exactly where God wanted me to be. Instantly, I fell on my knees in prayer and gratitude. "God, you are so amazing! How you planned this day before I was ever born. If only I would listen, I would find happiness in you. Thank you, my Heavenly Father, for being patient and persistently calling me home. I am overwhelmed by your love!"

And yes, still today I remain overwhelmed—head over heels in love with God and the transformation within my soul. Twenty-three years have passed since this conversation, yet I thought of this moment again recently when I was asked to speak at St. Patrick's in Wareham, Massachussetts. Through these years, I have been blessed with countless invitations to serve, witness, and grow in my faith. Now, as a Director of Parish Ministries, I have the additional blessed opportunity to lead others to discover their gifts and follow God's lead. For me, it is the journey of a lifetime—one I joyously embrace and continuously seek each day.

Elizabeth Reardon *is Director of Parish Ministries for St. Paul and Resurrection Parishes in Hingham, MA, and for many years was a radio host. Her blog is called* Theology Is a Verb.

Learning to Love the Cross

Lisa Nicholas

"The more we embrace the Cross, the more we become one with Jesus."—Bl. Charles de Foucauld

When I look back to see how the Lord has been working all my life to draw me closer to Himself, I am reminded of a scene in *The Silver Chair*, one of C. S. Lewis's Narnia Chronicles: two children have been sent by Aslan (the Christ figure of Narnia) on a perilous quest to rescue the lost prince of Narnia. Aslan gives them instructions on how to complete their quest but, in the hardship of their journey, they get so tied up in their own discomfort that they forget to look for the signs he has told them to watch for. Only after much struggle and danger do they happen to look back over the way they have come; now they can see clearly that a series of troublesome trenches through which they have struggled are actually a message carved in the earth, spelling out one of Aslan's instructions for anyone to see who cares to look. What the children in the story couldn't see at the time is plain in hindsight—but they have left it almost until too late before they look back.

In hindsight, my own journey through life, much of it vexing and painful at the time, takes on a clear shape. That shape, carved into the path of my life, is the shape of the Cross, and the instruction it spells out: "This is the way; walk in it."

My Introduction to the Cross

I hardly realized it at the time, but I learned basic theology of the Cross at about the age of six. At that time, and for several years afterward, I was essentially unchurched. My parents were either indifferent to religion (my father) or suspicious of it (my mother). I, however, craved it. One summer I was allowed to attend Vacation Bible School with some Baptist neighbors, where I learned the song, "Jesus loves me, this I know, for the Bible tells me so." The Bible, at that time, was literally a closed book to me. The only Bible in our home was one my mother had been given as a girl, when she briefly attended the Lutheran church with a school chum. It had a zipper around the edge, with a brass pull tab in the shape of a cross. I used to sneak into the living room, where the Bible sat gathering dust on the lower shelf of an end-table, and unzip it to peer inside. It seemed wonderfully mysterious and I would have loved to know what it all meant. But I didn't want my mother to know

I had been snooping, so I zipped the cover shut and dusted it to remove my fingerprints.

At that time, when I was in first grade, a Catholic family lived across from us, with kids about the same ages as me and my brothers and sister. One day the girl, Donna, showed me through their house. On the coffee table in their living room sat a large family Bible, open for all the world to see. She told me they read it as a family every night. Then she took me into her parents' bedroom to show me a picture of a bearded, long-haired man kneeling in the woods at night, his hands clasped on a large rock while a stream of light fell on his face. He was God, Donna told me, but His name was Jesus. She pointed to the cross on the wall, which I noticed had a man nailed to it—that was Jesus, too. Later, when I told my mother that Donna's parents had a picture of God in their bedroom, she told me that was nonsense—God is invisible. Jesus was just a man. That was her opinion, but deep in my mind and heart I was putting together those two important facts: Jesus (Who is God) loves me, and He suffered and died on the Cross.

I was the only one of four children in our family who showed any interest in religion, but I didn't show it often, for fear of my mother's disdain. She believed religion was mind-control and didn't want anyone putting the wrong ideas in my head. But God must have known my desire (I'm sure He's the one who put it in my heart), because one day, when I was ten years old,

He worked a miracle. That was the only way I could explain how my mother, of all people, happened to ask me if I would like to attend Easter Mass with her at the neighboring parish. I'm sure I must have been speechless for a moment as I tried to figure out if this was a trick question, but I managed to stammer, "Yes! Uh, sure!"

What I didn't know (and realized only decades later) was that, from my mother's point of view, the quickest and best way to get the four of us kids out of the public schools and into the much better local parochial school was for our entire family to become Catholic and join the parish. Attending that Easter Mass was just the first step.

Whatever my mother's motives were, I knew God had a hand in it. So, our family received basic religious instruction and, a few months later, as I was beginning sixth grade, I was baptized, received my first Holy Communion, and began Confirmation class, all within a few days' time. As it turned out, there was no opening at the parish school in my grade, so I was prepared for Confirmation in Saturday morning CCD class, where I drank in everything Sister Ignatius could teach us. I was thrilled to be confirmed the following spring, when the bishop told us we were now soldiers of Christ, a vocation I couldn't wait to live out.

My Cross to Bear

Unfortunately, my family was not destined to be "happy Catholics." My parents stop attending Mass almost immediately after my younger brother and sister were enrolled in the parochial school, and my older brother never went to Mass at all, that I can recall. Although my younger siblings and I continued to attend Mass on our own, as a family we were sham-Catholics.

Even that pretense was abandoned when we moved to Texas during my freshman year of high school, to a house in a neighborhood without a parochial school. My younger brother and sister went back into the public school system and my mother decreed that we would no longer be attending Mass. I said I could walk to Mass on my own—the church was right across from my school. But my mother forbade it and that ended the matter.

Those high school years were a sore trial for me, partly because I was being forced to live in exile from the Catholic Church. Also, our family problems were getting worse. My younger brother and sister were having difficulties at school, my older brother dropped out altogether, and my parents fought constantly. Meanwhile, I slid into a deep depression that I only began to climb out of after getting involved in the drama club at school during my junior year.

As things became more difficult at home, I implored God to help me hang on until I could leave home for college. God's response was clear: my family was my cross to bear. At the time, I didn't really understand what He meant by that—although I certainly found family life excruciating. I didn't want to bear them, I wanted to escape them.

One day, while digging through an old cigar box of mementos, I found a relic from my days as a happy young Catholic: a small crucifix that Sister Ignatius had given me as an award for being the star pupil of her Confirmation class. On the front, a mother-of-pearl inlay surrounded the figure of Christ on the Cross, and on the back were tiny Stations of the Cross, almost too small to recognize. I gazed at them and thought I understood a little of the pain of bearing a cross.

I was convinced that, once I got away from what I regarded as the toxic influence of my family and returned to the practice of my Catholic faith, my life would be much happier. I would be able to make new friends, grow closer to God, and discover my calling in life. I was in no hurry to get married, having seen how unhappy a bad marriage could be, but I longed for the close friendship of someone who really knew me and loved me as I was. I wasn't particularly career-oriented, but I hoped college would help me see how I could put my talents to work in a productive way that would be pleasing to God.

During college, I was very active in the Catholic community on the campus of my little liberal arts college. I did everything I could to deepen my knowledge and experience of the Catholic faith, despite the fact that our chaplain (a very kindly priest) seemed to think that we shouldn't be burdened by "too much religion" (a too-common attitude in the '70s). After all those years apart from the Church, I felt I had a lot of catching up to do. One of the things I was interested in was learning how to pray. I took part in a renewal program called Genesis II, which involved watching films of a priest talking about various aspects of the faith. It wasn't very inspiring, but I remember one detail that stayed with me—the priest in the films said that simply longing for God was itself a kind of prayer. About the same time, I found a book in the campus bookstore called *Closer than a Brother*, a modernization of *The Practice of the Presence of God* (Brother Lawrence), which was my introduction to the contemplative life and sharpened my hunger for a sense of God's presence in my life.

I graduated with a double major in English and Spanish with high honors. My academic prowess seemed to provide the only hint of how I could put my talents at God's service, so I followed my professors' advice and continued on to graduate school, accepting a doctoral fellowship in Comparative Literature at the University of Iowa. Overnight, I went from the comfortable environs of a tiny liberal arts college where I was a biggish fish in a small pond to a gigantic state university where I was a lonely minnow in a vast ocean.

Academically I did well and I learned to enjoy teaching, but in most ways those years in Iowa were the worst of my whole life. Although there was a Newman Center near campus, it wasn't geared toward graduate students and I had trouble connecting with other Catholics. My peers and professors in the Comp Lit program all thought it was weird that I went to church and "actually believed all that stuff." My loneliness grew and my morale sank lower and lower. I yearned more than ever for a sense of God's loving presence in my life.

I didn't tell my parents about my unhappiness—I wanted them to think I was doing well. All my siblings were having problems of their own, some of them quite serious, and I didn't want to be a failure. That's the way I felt—a failure. About to become a dropout. Useless. Friendless.

Then something happened, just as I was at my lowest, during Holy Week while I worshiped in the dingy basement chapel of the Newman Center. After the Holy Thursday liturgy, when the altar had been stripped and the Blessed Sacrament removed to a makeshift side altar decorated with flowering plants, in imitation of the Garden of Gethsemane, the priest invited us to stay and keep watch with the Lord during His hour of agony. I literally could not leave—I remained in my seat, praying and weeping tears that I could not stop. At midnight the priest returned to lock up for the night, but I would have stayed all night if he had allowed it.

The next day I returned for the Good Friday liturgy. When it came time to venerate the Cross, two young men carried in large beams of fresh timber, which they dropped with a horrible clatter onto the floor at the head of the center aisle. I still remember how the sound of hammer blows ricocheted like gunshots from the linoleum tile when they nailed the beams together to make a cross for our veneration. I felt I could almost see Jesus nailed there and, when I went forward to kiss the bare Cross, I could almost sense Jesus' bloody feet beneath my lips. I staggered away from the chapel afterward overwhelmed, and spent the next twenty-four hours in seclusion, trying to understand the experience.

Sometime on Holy Saturday, I pulled out a laminated prayer card that a high school friend, who was preparing to be an Episcopal priest, had sent me after I wrote to him about my troubles. On the card was the story/parable of "Footprints in the Sand." In a dream, a Christian looks back and sees the course of his life as two sets of footprints on a beach, side by side. "Why are there two sets of prints?" he asks the Lord, and Jesus replies, "Because I was always there with you, even when you didn't realize it." Then the man notices that at the darkest moments of his life there is only one set of prints, and he complains to the Lord: "How could you leave me alone at the darkest, most difficult moments of my life?" The Lord replies, "Precious one, I have never deserted you and I never will. Where you see only one set of prints, that is when I carried you."

I understood then that, while I was longing for the friendship of Christ, He had been there with me all along. Far from being indifferent to my suffering, He had made my suffering His own. I knew that, whatever lay ahead for me, He would be with me and He wanted me to be with Him. But it would not always be easy, because it would be the Way of the Cross.

Part of God's Family

Through the decades since that time, I've had to suffer many hardships and disappointments, and I've often repeated what St. Teresa of Avila once said to God: "If this is the way You treat Your friends, it's no wonder You have so few of them." And yet, God has fulfilled every desire He placed in my heart while I was young.

Shortly after that spring in Iowa City, He brought me back to Texas and introduced me to a little parish where I learned the richness of the Catholic faith, not just in formal doctrine but as it is lived out, day by day, through the Church's liturgical year, with its alternating seasons of penitence, celebration, and "ordinary" time. It was there that I learned to pray, not only with the Church but also in the secret of my heart. And it was there, too, that I learned, as Blessed Charles de Foucauld (also known as Brother Charles of the Cross) said, "The more we embrace the Cross, the more we become one with Jesus."

That small parish became my "parish family," the Christian family I had yearned for as a child; for many years it was the family to which I devoted myself wholeheartedly, as I would have liked to have done with my own parents and siblings. But, like any family, the parish was not made up of perfect people nor was it always free from quarrels and misunderstandings, disappointments and estrangements. Sometimes my own contributions went unnoticed, unappreciated, or even thwarted. Gradually, though, I learned to give without looking for recognition or counting the cost; gradually my "love offerings" to God through my parish were purified of my pride and hurt feelings.

Learning to love sacrificially in service to my parish helped prepare me to bear other crosses in my life: in my employment, in my health, in my personal aspirations and relationships. And, finally, life brought me to the cross that God had assigned to me when I was still a teenager.

This happened about ten years ago. I was teaching at a university in southern Indiana when a series of catastrophes occurred in my life that stripped me of almost everything I had, in worldly terms: my job, my health, my savings, even my possessions. Sick, exhausted, unemployed, and demoralized, I returned to Texas where, for the first time in more than thirty years, I found myself living with my parents—a situation that I thought represented the lowest point in my adult life.

Ever since I left for college, my mother had regarded me as the one who had "deserted" the family, and it is true that even after I moved back to Texas I spent little time hanging around the homestead, preferring my independence and the life I shared with my parish family. But, for the next twenty-five years, I was the one who stayed put while the others wandered off on their own. My younger brother and sister each migrated to the west coast in their early twenties and returned to Texas only when their personal situations demanded it; my parents traded their house for a motor home and spent nearly ten years on the move, settling down again in the Dallas area only when they began to need regular medical attention. By that time, they had come to prize their independence as much as any of us younger ones did. They had no intention of sharing their home with any of their children again. Moving in with them was literally the last thing that occurred to me when my own situation became dire.

As it happens, at that exact time, my parents' lives were also reaching a crisis. My father, already in his eighties, suffered a series of health catastrophes that neither he nor my mother was equipped to handle. They needed help as much as I did. God used this "perfect storm" of troubles to bring us back together as a family.

Learning to Embrace the Cross

Thus, my "temporary" stay with them became permanent. Putting aside my own problems, I helped my mother deal with my father's declining health and growing dementia, giving her the relief she badly needed so that she could relax a bit after a lifetime of worry. That was also the period when the rest of our family was slowly being drawn back together ,as my scattered siblings returned to Texas. Soon we found ourselves all living within a couple of miles of one another for the first time since we were kids.

Although I never married or had a family of my own—another cross I've had to bear—I now find myself the practical support of my surviving parent and siblings. As I write this, all three of my siblings are disabled physically and mentally; my father has passed into eternity (which I pray is a blessed one with the Lord); my mother, due to her frail health, relies on me for daily help, cooking her meals and assisting her with personal tasks.

I have finally learned what the Lord meant when he whispered in my heart forty years ago that "my family is the cross I have to bear." He didn't mean, "Well, you simply have to put up with them, like it or lump it"; He meant, "This is the way you must show your love for them, by bearing with them patiently, as I did with those who persecuted Me and put Me to death, by clinging to the Cross for their sake. This is the way you draw close to Me. This is the way I will prepare you for Eternity."

I have come to love my family more than I ever did as a child, and I've learned that God is always giving me what I need rather than what I think I need. The loss of so many vestiges of my former life—a hard cross at the time—has become a kind of freedom to put myself at the Lord's disposal in ways I had never imagined; so, in that way, embracing my cross has allowed me to die to my old life and rise to a new one with Christ.

My life has been full of adventures and struggles but, as I look back now, this is what I see: with all its stumblings and turnings, the path of my life spells out the beautiful message of the Cross: "Love one another as I have loved you." Thanks be to God, I am still learning just what that means.

Lisa Nicholas *is a member of the Ordinariate parish of St. Mary the Virgin in Arlington, TX, where she has served in many capacities over the past three and a half decades. After earning a Ph. D. in Literature from the University of Dallas, she taught for a number of years in Indiana and Texas. Now she lives on a lake shore at the edge of Dallas where she writes, translates, and edits Catholic authors at Mitey Editing.*

Deep Awakening

Karl Erickson

THE DEPARTURE OF my wife and me from the Protestant tradition was a reflection of God's leading hand and presence in our lives. Unknown to us at the time, each spiritual step we took prepared us in some new way for our ultimate destination of the Catholic Church. Before discussing six key points that convinced us to journey across the Tiber, I think it is important to examine some of the most personal influences that affected our course.

I was raised in the Church of the Nazarene, a Protestant church of the Wesleyan tradition. My mother, a single parent, sacrificed greatly to enroll me at a Catholic grade school in the fourth grade, and I stayed in Catholic schools for the following six years. It was not easy to be one of the few Protestants in a Catholic school, and it took some time before I realized that the teasing and bullying I experienced on the playground had less to do with my religious affiliations and more to do with the fact that I simply stood out. Being the class clown probably didn't help the situation!

Even though times were not easy, I found myself immediately drawn to the Mass. I remember being extremely embarrassed and hurt when one of the teachers pulled me out of the Communion line one morning after she realized I was not Catholic. No one had explained the Communion restriction to me. (This experience was seen by some of the students as a signal for open season on Protestant students.) While it was not a happy time, I kept feeling a strange tug from the Mass. In a way, I think I wanted to belong to the Church at an early age.

My grandfather, a retired minister with the Christian and Missionary Alliance, was a devout and God-fearing man. I always listened to what he had to say concerning the Bible and issues of the Church. One element of the church service that always bothered him greatly was the transition away from the old hymns to more modern musical "performances" and simple-minded choruses. His concerns instilled in me an early understanding that the service was veering away from worship and moving toward entertainment. There was little in the way of reverence for "the Man Upstairs." The church service seemed to convey his majesty and mystery less and less. Something important was lost when we failed to recognize or acknowledge the awesome majesty of our Creator.

In fact, it was on a fishing trip with my grandfather one sunny afternoon as a young child that I committed my life to Christ and experienced what Catholics call "the second conversion." It was an important step that sparked my desire to serve God and go where he directed me. It was my grandfather who first impressed upon me the need to listen to God's voice and study the Word. To my grandfather, God was always near and welcoming. The fishing might not have been that terrific, but I knew that God had caught me, and that was good enough.

Fast-forward a few years, and I married Kimberly Collier, whom I met in a New Testament class at our alma mater, Seattle Pacific University (a Free Methodist University). The college years were spent in late Seattle walks and a great deal of time in thought and contemplation. My first experience in a religion class was a definite eye-opener.

From the beginning of our marriage, finding a church that seemed right was a struggle. We visited church after church and spent significant time in prayer on the issue. This was not what we had planned. I had always expected to settle down quickly in the "perfect church" home, but we just could not find it.

At times, we wondered whether we were just too picky. Kimberly was raised in a denomination very similar to the Nazarene Church in which I was raised, but we never could discover a church home where we both felt a continued sense of belonging or purpose. For me, the issue of reverence became more and more important.

I just could not accept a church service that came across more like entertainment than worship. From Lutheran and Baptist to Episcopal, we visited more denominations than we could count.

The Episcopal Church—Not!

After years of searching, we discovered the Episcopal Church in Salem, Oregon. The minister at that time was a gifted preacher, and we felt that perhaps we had finally found where we belonged. We soon became involved in various ministries through the church. All was proceeding very well until the Episcopal Church of the USA decided to ordain an openly gay man as bishop. The Episcopal Church took this low road in August of 2003, and we soon realized that we could not stay within a denomination that took this grievous misstep. It made an especially deep impression when the church leadership asserted that the Holy Spirit had led them to this decision. Many of us came to a different conclusion.

So, much to our frustration, our "church shopping" began anew. Then, it happened—one morning we just decided to attend a Catholic Mass. We had been driving past this particular church in our neighborhood for years, but we had never taken the time to visit. The plan was to just to make a quick stop, then continue our church quest. To our surprise, however, the Mass blew us away. It was beautiful, and the message from the priest was powerful and filled with deep meaning for us.

We weren't quite ready to admit that this was where we belonged, however, so after attending an early Mass, we took the kids in tow and visited a Free Methodist service across town. With the beautiful Mass still fresh in my memory, the anti-Catholic sermon during the Methodist service made me all but storm out of the church. My wife recalls sitting on our back porch later that day and being so miserable that the thought of starting her own church passed through her mind. She was stunned when she realized how destructive this line of thinking could have been. Soon, we both seriously began to consider converting to the Catholic Church.

The first part of our spiritual journey was all about being led to the Catholic Church. The next part of our spiritual awakening concerned deep study of Scripture, the *Catechism of the Catholic Church*, and the writings of the Church Fathers. My father-in-law, John Collier, was a major help to us at this point. John Collier is the fine artist and sculptor who created the Catholic Memorial at Ground Zero in New York City. John was able to answer many of our questions and concerns regarding the Catholic Church. When a question stumped him, he would put us into contact with priests or others who could answer our many concerns. After a time, we were surprised to realize that all of our stumbling blocks had been removed and that many issues that we thought were insurmountable turned out to be simple differences in vocabulary or new perspectives. Whether through John or our RCIA program, God surrounded us with knowledgeable people to answer those troubling questions.

Six areas were pivotal in my acceptance of the Catholic Church as the one and true Church established by Jesus Christ and entrusted to the first pope, Saint Peter. Some were more of a hurdle than others, but they all held important meaning along our journey.

1. Sola Scriptura

Sola Scriptura, or the idea that Christian authority is vested in Scripture alone, was pretty easily sent on its way. Do we accept that each person must interpret every Scripture passage on his own? This seemed to be sending our Episcopalian friends toward moral entropy. How can the Holy Spirit be guiding different churches in opposite interpretative directions regarding identical Scripture passages? We felt there must be an authority somewhere to assist church members in understanding the Bible, because the moral anchors were certainly breaking loose within many Protestant denominations.

2. Birth Control

With the Anglican acceptance of birth control at the Lambeth Conference in 1930, and the brief Protestant love affair with eugenics, we are left with Protestant denominations that recognize abortion as a grave sin, but they don't see the moral similarity between birth control and abortion. Every other denomination is blown by the winds of social and cultural change. Granted, some great Evangelical thinkers such as Amy Laura Hall are starting to ask the tough questions, but where is the consistency of reason and truth most readily found in regards to the Culture of Death, which is tearing our world apart—spiritually, morally, and demographically?

3. The Papacy

Non-Catholics frequently misunderstand and misconstrue the value and purpose of our pope. As we learned, Catholics don't believe that everything the pope utters is infallible. We are not bound, for example, to follow his personal preferences. Only when the pope speaks *ex cathedra* does the Catholic Church take his statements as infallible, and this has happened only two or three times in the life of the Church. Furthermore, this does not represent trust in the pope so much as it represents trust that God won't permit his Church to fall into error. More and more Protestant churches appear to be heading straight for moral relativism, as gravely warned against by the great Anglican writer, C. S. Lewis.

4. Christian Unity

The Bible repeatedly calls us to unity. Did we have sufficient reason to stay apart from the Catholic Church? How should we prefer that the mystical Body of Christ be divided so many thousands of times in the different denominations of the day? The Protestant churches seem like injured cells endlessly dividing and replicating themselves. This division is precisely what Saint Paul was warning Christians to avoid, so that we might reflect Christian unity to the world. We should all consider ourselves members of a broken family, and it's time we came back together.

5. The Real Presence

Before joining the Catholic Church, Kimberly and I always insisted upon a literal interpretation of Scripture, but we balked at applying a literal interpretation to John 6, which describes the Eucharist as the actual Body and Blood of Christ. It seems that the disciples were deeply troubled by our Lord's words. If it was a symbol alone, it would not have been a challenging teaching at all, and Jesus would have clarified his meaning to the disciples. In fact, if his followers had so badly misunderstood, it would have been unlike Jesus to refrain from a deeper explanation of something so critical and central to our Christian walk. Nowhere in Scripture is the Eucharistic mystery characterized as a symbol, and the early Church did not treat it as symbolic in nature. The early Church Fathers also recognized the Real Presence as central in their understanding of the Eucharist. We were convinced.

6. Mary

Who is Mary? When my wife and I were studying in preparation to join the Catholic Church, the concept of Mary was one of the hardest ideas to get our minds around. Coming from the Evangelical tradition, we found that most of the new concepts we learned were simply a result of a more logical and consistent interpretation of Scripture. Although the verses are clearly there, understanding Mary required something beyond Biblical interpretation, and it was not easy. Slowly it began to make sense, and I recognized that praying to Mary was not the same as worshiping Mary. Instead, it was more along the lines of talking to a close and respected friend.

When my eyes were opened to the truth of Mary, I was profoundly grateful for the opportunity to see her clearly for who she was and is today. This Catholic understanding of Mary hinges on accepting her as the new Eve. Where Eve disobeyed God's call, Mary listened attentively and obeyed in a spirit of selfless love. As Protestants, we might have carelessly declared many of these Marian beliefs to be meaningless extra-Biblical concepts that have no value to Christianity. But there are core beliefs that all Christians share, which are likewise not clearly defined in the Bible. The Trinity, for instance, is never spelled out in so many words, but its truth is made abundantly clear through a careful reading of the Bible and the wisdom of the saints who came before us. We were learning about tradition.

In conversations with skeptical Protestants, I often explain the Catholic perspective this way. Their tradition is like an artist's canvas, which contains all the necessary artistic elements in the foreground. The background, however, lies bare of color or shape, simply white canvas awaiting the painter's brush. The Catholic Church, on the other hand, is a canvas of rich and vibrant colors, which seem to leap from the painting. Other Christians could be so enriched if they caught sight of the second painting and drank in its rich meaning, a perfect dovetailing of faith and reason. May God open all our friends' eyes to this great beauty. As John Collier recently described this fullness of faith, "It was as if I had been worshiping in the basement all my life and got to move into the sanctuary."

Our departure from the Protestant tradition was a reflection of God's leading hand and presence in our lives. It was less a conversion than it was enrichment and a blessing from God to see the beautiful complexity of our faith. Each spiritual step we took prepared us in some new way for our ultimate destination of the Catholic Church. As my wife and I sat beside my dying grandmother in a hospital room overlooking the bright tapestry of autumn colors spread out below, I was comforted by the fact that we serve the same God and Savior, Jesus Christ. Still, I am thankful to have come home to the fullness found only within the Catholic Church.

I remember my first Confession and a mysteriously fragrant breeze. Later, I learned that scents and gardens traditionally are associated with some of the most powerful conversion stories—e.g., Saint Augustine recalled being drawn to God again in the quiet solitude of his garden. Upon exiting the confessional, an inexplicable cool breeze of a pine forest brushed by my face, and I knew that this was God's wonderful way of welcoming me to his Church, which teaches reverence and honor for God at every turn. It's good finally to be home.

Karl Erickson *is the author of several books and more than eighty articles, appearing in publications such as* America, The National Catholic Weekly, *and* This Rock. *He has worked as an Oregon state employee for more than two decades. In 2018, Karl graduated with a BA in English Literature and New Media from Marylhurst University.*

Finding Jesus in the Eucharist

Greg Wasinski

As a lifelong Catholic, I spent many years going through the motions of Mass, catechism class, sacramental preparation, and prayer, without allowing myself to appreciate the beauty of our faith. For a time as an adult, I even drifted away from going to church altogether. Often, even when I was present, I had zero realization of, or respect for, the Real Presence of Jesus Christ in the Eucharist.

I allowed myself to be disconnected. I didn't desire to encounter him and accept his unconditional love found in his sacrifice and resurrection in the Eucharist. I didn't appreciate the gift before me in the person of our Savior. Little did I know that his Body and Blood would become my point of conversion back to the faith I was baptized into. A fall morning Mass in Ordinary Time changed everything for me—not what I believed, but what I experienced.

I took my seat in the third row near the choir, which I'd been settling into for the past three years since I made my return to church. I was attending Mass because my wife had convinced me the kids needed the example of their father, if we were going to raise them Catholic. You could have called me an unwilling participant.

However, this day, instead of mentally checking out and simply being physically present, my attention remained on the words being offered throughout the entire liturgy. It was during the Eucharistic Prayer, at the moment when Christ's Body, Blood, Soul, and Divinity take the place of bread and wine, that I began to cry. "Holy tears," as I would later learn they are called, flowed from my eyes, trickling down my cheeks.

Maybe for the first time ever, I realized Christ was in front of me in the Eucharist. There he was, for me, accepting me as I was: present but so distant, broken but loved.

There were no lightning bolts or shaking of the Earth at the instant I noticed him. Instead, there was a gentle peace. Our Lord connected with me at that moment to snap me out of the apathy I had allowed to consume me.

In a second, my road to conversion took a turn I never expected. When I received him in Holy Communion that day, I knew there was something different and I was being remade. This was not the first time he showed up in the Eucharist; it was just the first time I was willing to embrace him.

He had been calling to me since the day of my birth,

but I had shut our Lord out. I took the riches of faith that were being offered and shoved them aside for worldly things that could never fulfill me. In a way, you could say it was this "Prodigal Son" moment that finally made me feel "at home" in his presence. He embraced me in the Eucharist, and I never wanted to let go ever again.

Conversion of the heart takes place through the Holy Spirit when we stop running from what is true and allow our entire being to recognize Christ's love; in this case, for me, it's the source and summit of our Catholic faith found in the Eucharist.

There weren't hundreds of changes I needed to make in my life to find Jesus in the Eucharist. I didn't have to go back to school, nor did I need to memorize specific Scripture verses. I needed to allow Christ into places in myself I was never willing to expose before. I had to be brave enough to surrender everything I was holding back in my heart from God.

By offering myself, I became aware how much he was offering me. I began to feel his presence and then allow everything he was and is to consume every part of me from the moment I received Holy Communion.

We can walk away from a lot of things in religion, even dismiss the everyday faith and real-life moments that occur in the world around us. However, we cannot deny the moment we feel our heart come alive because we have found all of Christ in the Supper of the Lord.

If we begin to accept how deeply he wants to give himself unconditionally over and over in this sacrament, no matter what happens or where we have been, nothing will ever be able to tear us away from our Catholic faith.

***Greg Wasinski** is an internationally recognized Catholic inspirational speaker and author from Cleveland, OH. His latest book is* Unconditionally: Finding Jesus in the Eucharist. *He also offers his radio talents as a daily contributor to SiriusXM Radio's Catholic Channel with his "Faith and Real Life Moments."*

My Restless Heart

Cyndi Lucky

"O God, our hearts are restless until they can find rest in you."
St. Augustine

I WAS BORN and raised in Dallas, Texas, in a predominately Southern Baptist home. My two loving parents adopted me at birth. My daddy was a devoted Southern Baptist, and my mother was an inactive Lutheran. I found out about my adoption at age nine and never gave it much thought, except that my parents definitely wanted me.

As I matured, I became more and more independent, but less and less involved with my dad's church. Through a close friend, I got involved at a church with a strong youth group. There, I accepted Jesus as my personal Savior and was baptized at about age thirteen or fourteen. I spent a few years very involved there and got to know Jesus in a personal way.

Sadly, at about age sixteen, after my dad's near-death experience, I disengaged from my church, God, and Jesus. My mother had become increasingly emotionally incapable of mothering me, due to a prescription drug she took for her acute asthma. I became disenchanted with the "unorganized" organized religion I'd been active in. My expectations may have been too high, but as a sixteen-year-old I expected support from friends and church members that just wasn't there. The further I got from the community, the further I fell away from God. I still believed; I just quit following.

I entered into a thirty-year journey through a desert full of sin and self-destructive behavior. During this time, I thought I had it all under control. I bounced from man to man. I partied frequently and heavily. When I was twenty-seven, I lost my mother after a six-week hospital stay in ICU. After her passing, I spiraled downward even further, feeling a lot of guilt for my part in our difficult relationship.

About a year before my adoptive mother passed away, I had found my birth mom. I was surprised by her story. I had always taken for granted that my adoption probably was a result of a teen pregnancy. Far from it. She had been in an adulterous affair in a small town with a married man who had two children. In 1960, abortion was still illegal and she was afraid of the back-alley butchers who performed abortions, so she came to Dallas to deliver and put me up for adoption.

The Lord obviously had his mighty and protecting hand on my life since conception. He protected me from abortion and from being raised as an illegitimate child in an alcoholic environment with little or no religious affiliation. Through my adoption, he put me in the loving and tender care of a couple who not only desperately wanted a child but also made sure I was introduced to Jesus and God.

I married and divorced numerous times. My children's father was Catholic. Because of his mother's devout faith in the Church, not only did I agree to raise them Catholic but I fell in love with the Church. I loved the peace I felt when I attended Mass with them. I felt reengaged with the Lord. I felt his presence there, even though I didn't understand the Eucharist yet. I entered RCIA twice but, because both of us had prior marriages, I was unable to receive the Sacraments.

After my last divorce, during my son's Confirmation, I heard the Lord tell me, "It's time." I was sitting in a folding chair in our new church, watching all these young people commit their lives to Christ through the Sacrament of Confirmation, and yet I was still unable to receive Communion with my child at an important time for him. I had spent thirteen years raising two children in Catholic school and had never received Communion with them. I felt like the Lord was telling me to see that my son's soul was in better condition than mine. What a shame, I'd wasted so much time!

I had a beautiful friend in the Catholic school's extended day program, who just happened to be the Director of Family Ministry and the RCIA facilitator at the time. She had told me she would help me through the process and that someday "they'd get me."

They say that nothing can be healed until it's brought out into the Light. My experience going through the annulment process was one of healing and forgiveness, but I also learned what had been missing from my life and my marriages. Answering the questions for the tribunal brought those wounds and sin into the light of God's Holy Church for healing and most of all forgiveness—not just for the offenses against me, but also the offenses I myself was guilty of. I had to forgive myself first, and then the rest came much easier. Acknowledging my part of the failures was the first step. I am thankful for the Church's guidance during that process.

A little less than a year after I was moved at my son's Confirmation, I was confirmed myself. I was received into the Church at Easter Vigil, 2007, under the Confirmation name of St. Augustine. When it came time to choose, I didn't know much about many of the saints, but I'd heard bits and pieces about Augustine's "worldly" life before his conversion. The little information I had about him let me know that, given my past, anything was possible with me, also. The Lord has blessed me with an incredible husband and a marriage validated by the Church. My journey has led me from leading a women's group for five years into a ministry of love, evangelization, and knowledge working for Dr.

Marcellino D'Ambrosio, one of the best Catholic speakers of our time. I have traveled and brought my daughter on a pilgrimage in the Holy Land with Dr. D'Ambrosio, have attended many Catholic events and been blessed with meeting many of God's servants. We have been in the company of holiness through the Crossroads Initiative and Mary Immaculate Church, which also brought my husband into the Church at the Easter Vigil, 2016.

I had a void in my life for thirty years and tried to fill it with just about everything the Church and Sacred Scripture warns us about. Only One could fill it with the love and tenderness my heart desired.

Cyndi Lucky *is a native Texan, proud of her roots in Oak Cliff, a suburb of Dallas. She worked for the Crossroads Initiative for four years, after volunteering for one year.*

In Loving Pursuit of Our God

Marie Therese Kceif

MY CATHOLIC PARENTS raised me on a dairy farm in Wisconsin. We went to church weekly and frequented the Sacraments. My mother even brought us to a local farm wives' Bible study every week where we learned about God's Word. Though I had the tools to be confident in God's love for me, I allowed what others thought of me to define who I was, instead of his love for me. Being a shy, awkward, skinny, and undeveloped teenager, I struggled with what the world saw as beautiful instead of what God said was beautiful. I started to believe the Devil's lie whispered to me that I couldn't be popular or loved by God.

At college, I started to fill the void of wanting to be fully loved with other things. I packed my schedule with activities, boyfriends, and even premarital sex. I stopped going to Mass every Sunday and slowly challenged the healthy guidance and moral boundaries taught to me by the Church and my parents. I did not believe in the Real Presence of Jesus in Holy Communion. Because I didn't believe God could deeply love me, I had a problem believing he would have an active relationship with me. Perhaps this is similar to my feeling that I could never belong to the in-group at school, so I surely couldn't be in the group God loved either.

I actively pursued a career as a US Army active duty officer and pilot that would make me look prized by others. At first, it was a role I could handle and I found happiness in it. Soon, like all the other things in my life, it was not enough. I pursued a role suggested to me that was beyond my training. I listened to the pressure of what others thought and the worldly promise it provided instead of what God thought was best for me. Accepting the position of Apache Commander of the Calvary and Attack without the proper experience led me to a serious struggle in my life.

Because I always wanted to have a sense of belonging, I ended up in an affair with the top gun of our unit and became pregnant. I then divorced my husband, and remarried. I was asked to leave the military and my beloved career. When my new husband, who I thought loved me, started to abuse me physically, emotionally, and mentally, I ended up in the emergency room and he wound up in jail.

Because of his large debts and the debt we had incurred trying to make a new life, we filed for bankruptcy in just two years. He started to have an affair and wanted a divorce. Married only three years, we now had two boys together. I found myself a single mom of two small children without credit, status, or material goods.

Reaching Out to God

God allowed the lesser evil to work in the worse evil of my lukewarm heart. Losing everything, I found myself reaching out for help to the God I didn't think loved me.

Exhausted and broken-hearted, I called out to Jesus one morning before work. Hugging the family's big white Catholic Bible, I asked him, "Lord, where is there joy in my journey? If it weren't for the boys, I would just want to . . ." I cried for all that I had done, for my poor choices, for the hurt I had caused, and for the place I was left in.

That's all God needed. He showered down blessings and answered prayers: a car when I had no money nor credit to purchase one, a couch when I had no furniture, a Bible study when I knew nothing of them, good daycare for my children when I was at work, and countless other little bouquets of blessings. The answered prayers were so specific to my wants and needs that he showed me how he loved and cared about every aspect of my life.

As a result, he reintroduced me to Bible study groups, *lectio divina*, and a deeper prayer life so that I could hear and listen to him speak to me. He slowly showed me through visions, dreams, and miracles that he truly loved me and was there all the time. I received the grace to forgive my husband, seek an annulment, and reverse my tubal ligation.

As God's blessings continued, I found a home and was able to maintain my well-paying job to support our little family. After five years I came back with a passion to the full truth of the Catholic Church and God's healing. He brought a man into our life who loved my kids as his own and me as if I were his virgin bride. I am now happily married to my husband and spiritually to my Lord. I now follow God's lead, guiding Bible studies, speaking, writing, and many other things God brings along my path. I no longer let the world define who I am, but define myself by *whose* I am.

Marie Therese Kceif *holds a Bachelor of Science degree in Mathematics and has been a US Army Captain as well as an attack helicopter pilot and commander, automotive manager, Bible study leader, RCIA guide, lector, speaker, writer, wife, and mom. She is the author of* Eve's Apple *and lives with her husband in Yokohama, Japan, where she ministers at her church and teaches English classes.*

“I Make All Things New”

Colleen Spiro

“And he who sat on the throne said,
‘Behold, I make all things new.’” (Revelation 21:5)

WHEN I WAS a child, I loved going to the Protestant church in our small New England town. I especially loved going on the first Sunday of the month when we received Communion. Our church taught that Communion was only a symbol of Jesus’ Body and Blood. I never understood what it all meant, but I somehow knew it was special. Over the years, my family drifted away from church, and I attended only sporadically. But when I did go, I still loved to receive Communion. I didn’t know why. I just followed my heart.

When I met my husband, Rich, he was a divorced, non-practicing Catholic. We didn’t attend church but had many discussions about faith and God. Rich cleared up a lot of my misunderstandings about Catholicism. After we got married, my father-in-law kept praying that I would convert, but I had no interest at that time.

After our second son was born, Rich decided to get an annulment of his first marriage. When the annulment was granted, we remarried in the Catholic Church and started attending Mass. At first, I wasn't very comfortable. I went to church because I wanted my husband to be happy, and I thought it was a good thing to do for our boys.

Gradually, I became more comfortable going to Mass, though I felt left out because I couldn't receive the Sacraments. Soon I had a nagging feeling that God was asking me to make more of a commitment. One day, in the middle of Mass, I knew what that meant. I knew, without any doubt, that I wanted to be Catholic.

My yearning for God and his Church seemed to come out of the blue, but it was real. I felt his love drawing me to him. I will never forget the surprised look on Rich's face when I told him I wanted to take the classes to become Catholic. And I remember the moment when I knew I'd made the right decision. It was at the class on the Eucharist. As the priest explained the Real Presence of Jesus, tears ran down my cheeks. This is what I had been unconsciously searching for since childhood. The symbol of Jesus had not been enough for me. I had yearned for the real Jesus and I found him in the Catholic Church. I found him in the Eucharist. And I believed.

More than twenty-eight years ago, I became a Catholic at the Easter Vigil Mass. When I received the Body and Blood of Jesus for the first time, I knew I was home.

I have experienced many changes since then. My husband is now a permanent deacon in the Catholic Church. I am a spiritual director, a Benedictine oblate, and a parish secretary. I write about faith and the spiritual life. I can hardly recognize myself when I look back at my life and see how much it has changed.

As I look back at my conversion, I realize that over time the Holy Spirit had been changing my heart, slowly but surely, day by day. And then, when I began to attend Mass and I heard God's Word over and over, my heart softened and opened up.

And all things became new.

Colleen Spiro, *a convert, mother, and grandmother, is married to a permanent deacon. A Benedictine oblate and certified spiritual director, Colleen loves to share her faith and encourage others through her retreats and writings. She blogs at Catholic Prayer Life and presents podcasts at Finding God in the Everyday.*

God Bless the Unbroken Road

Neil Combs

MANY FAITH JOURNEYS and conversion stories are filled with trials and conflict, with obstacles and hesitance—a "broken road," as they say. My road, though fairly long and winding, isn't so broken. I'm not saying that I've never had any spiritual struggles—I've had a few. The most notable one was my family's move from Long Island to Rochester, NY, during a difficult time in our marriage. This simple change of jobs was supposed to end in Syracuse but that didn't work out, so we scrambled to make a move to Rochester with the same company. I didn't even know where Rochester was! Then we couldn't find a house in the area where we were looking. I was fighting God at every turn because I had a plan and he wasn't cooperating!

As it turns out, God's plan was way better than mine. We've never been better, and the move ultimately resulted in my conversion to the Catholic faith. My road has been an intellectual journey. But let me start closer to the beginning.

I was born on Long Island in Oceanside, NY, in a Lutheran home, the faith of my father. We attended a wonderful Lutheran church there, and I attended youth group with most of the people I would (and still do) call best friends. I learned to appreciate my Christian faith early in life and was usually fairly close to the church. When I was 19, I met a girl who would become my wife almost six years later. Mary was and is a devout Catholic. While we dated, we attended both my Lutheran church and her Catholic church in Oceanside, sometimes going to Mass and sometimes going to "church." As time went on, we went a bit more often to her church, St. Anthony's, where eventually we were married. Attending the two churches, I noticed many similarities in the services and didn't give much thought to which church we attended.

When we had children, we brought them up in the Catholic faith, since we were attending the Catholic Church more regularly. I started to notice a few differences from my Lutheran faith (which I hadn't truly let go of) but not enough to make me do anything other than becoming more attentive. I think I had an intellectual understanding of God, but not an emotional one. I didn't have that "personal relationship" I hear people talk about. I continued to attend Mass and "follow the leader": sit, stand, kneel, sit. I still struggled with my faith.

I can't say I lived a life of virtue, even in front of my family. I may have appeared virtuous, maybe even holy, from the outside, but I had a dark side that I rarely brought out in front of others. Let's just say my morals were a bit askew for much of my life. My wife once said to me that sometimes I treated the people from church better than my family, and that hurt. But she was probably right—no, she was definitely right.

In 1999, at the age of thirty-seven, I got a bit of a wake-up call. I had a partial blockage in a coronary artery, which required the insertion of a stent. I felt very vulnerable at that time. My marriage was struggling because of my behavior and my bad choices. I couldn't seem to put my wife first consistently; it was all about me. This was when my company "asked" me to take the job in Syracuse. You know, the one that ended up in Rochester (actually Hilton, a tiny suburb.) And it brought us to that tiny town's small Catholic Church, the Church of St. Leo the Great. They were so welcoming that I took notice. It felt comfortable—almost Lutheran.

By the time our children were ready for Confirmation, I had grown a lot in my faith through reading books and Scripture and listening to radio and CDs. I was learning more about what the Church taught, rather than what I thought it taught. I had to admit to myself that it made a lot of sense. So I decided to go through the RCIA program in our current parish, St. Leo's in Hilton, NY, and to enter the Catholic Church with my kids. There were no skyrockets or major transformations, but I had become a Catholic. Emotionally, it felt right. Intellectually, it made sense.

I didn't have a lot of preconceptions about the Catholic Church, but those that I had melted away quickly with sound and logical explanations. I appreciated the continuity and unwavering strength of the Church. And it was such a great feeling to go through the Sacraments of Reconciliation and the Eucharist at the same time as my kids. That is something we will always share. My wife was overjoyed, because we had become a happy Catholic family. I soon began working with our youth ministry program and was teaching high school teens.

About a year later, the biggest catalyst of my faith life occurred: I went on a retreat called Cursillo. There I learned more about my faith and my role in the church as a member of the laity, realizing that we are all a part of the Church and that sharing Christ was up to priests, as well as the deacons and us laity. I had time to pray and talk with Jesus, and it hit me clearly: I didn't talk to Jesus nearly enough. I didn't have a relationship with him. Oh, I prayed—*telling* him what I needed and asking for help—but I never listened for him to talk to me. When I began my relationship with my wife, I spent all kinds of time with her, sharing feelings and failures, yet I hadn't given God that same part of me. But that weekend I prayed. I poured my heart out to Jesus in a way I had never imagined possible, like I was talking and crying with a dear friend.

That began a three-year voyage to learn about and understand prayer, leading me to do something I'd never dreamed I'd do: write a book on what I learned. *A Body in Prayer* is really about having a deep relationship with Christ and including him in our daily life. In a way, the writing was a big part of my heart's conversion. As I spent more time with Christ, I was also studying more about my newfound Catholic faith and listening to CDs. The more I learned, the more sense it made and the more I loved it. I realized the genius of Catholicism. It all made sense, and it all fit together. And it all came down to having (and living) that relationship with Christ. When I wrote *A Body in Prayer,* it was a retelling of the relationship I'd developed with Christ. I started to include him in my whole day by making decisions about what I watched, what I read, what I listened to. The amazing strength I experienced fasting just one day a week gave me the love I experienced through time in adoration, and I felt the joy and satisfaction of reaching out to those in need.

I love my Lutheran roots because they taught me to love Christ and to go out into the world to bring his message to others through my actions. I don't think of my journey as a conversion, but as more of a progression. I believe my early faith has gotten me to the place where I am now. Some people may have been surprised that I became Catholic and may even feel that I made a mistake. To them I say: don't worry, it was a well-thought-out, rational decision made along my unbroken road.

***Neil Combs** is a pharmacist and the author of* A Body in Prayer. *Neil is active in the youth ministry, Knights of Columbus, and the worship band, Hearts Ablaze, at St. Leo the Great parish in Hilton, NY. He and his wife Mary teach Pre-Cana classes and work in social justice and other ministries. His website is A Body in Prayer.*

Two Living Encounters

Sr. Anne Marie Walsh, SOLT

I GREW UP IN the '60s and '70s, attending Catholic grade and high schools run by the School Sisters of St. Francis. The Sisters all wore habits down to the floor and, from the time I was little, I felt there was some mysterious personal connection between the Sisters and me. A few Sisters weren't kind, and I saw some real displays of temper, but so many of the Sisters communicated genuine love. I always felt that I was going to be a Sister.

Then all the changes came and I watched the Sisters go from habits to street clothes. Soon they were out the door, leaving their vocations behind. Then the priests begin changing as well. They said things that seemed out of keeping with their dignity as priests, and many of them, too, left their vocations.

By the time I was finished with high school, I was pretty disillusioned. I stopped practicing and living my faith. I never stopped believing in God, but I stopped going to Mass and stopped praying.

I began searching to find real love. I observed that love is the one thing that changes people. When people are in love, it transforms them. They become good, kind, happy, less selfish, more willing to bear hardship for the good. I wanted to live that way.

For eight years, I looked for love at the human level. But the state of relationships around me was frightening. I felt pain at the things some of my girlfriends did that demeaned their dignity.

I noticed that a lot of men had a hard time committing. I would look at a man and wonder if he could be a good father, or if he would be too centered in himself for the sacrifice required to be a good father and husband. I feared to be with someone who would be faithful for about five years and then that would be it. I didn't think I would be able to bear infidelity, because I was looking for real love, a love that would sacrifice itself completely for the other. That's how I wanted to give myself.

This was a dark time for me emotionally and psychologically, with a lot of interior pain, depression, desolation, loneliness, and confusion. Now I understand that it was partly due to my leaving a state of grace, because once I came back into grace, my interior peace and hopefulness returned. I felt light again, able to receive healing, able to understand life with a clarity that gave it meaning I couldn't find outside of grace. I needed to be jarred back to the Truth.

After college, I taught for about four years, until I was knocked out of my dream world and into reality. I had to experience a death in a relationship to understand I was never going to find what I was looking for on a solely human level.

I was in the midst of deep interior pain when, one Saturday afternoon, when I was alone doing dishes at the kitchen sink, I suddenly felt the presence of Our Lady next to me. It was so natural that I wasn't alarmed. I couldn't see her, but I could feel her. I knew she was there, and I wasn't afraid. It seemed like a normal thing. Nothing went through my head, like, "How could this be? You haven't even been praying for the last eight years, let alone going to Church." No discomfort, no self-consciousness; I was completely at ease.

And so I started talking to her, interiorly, because I knew somehow I was supposed to tell her what was in my heart. I said to her, "If I can't be in love, then I don't see the meaning of life." Then, from somewhere deep within my spirit, deeper than just thought, I said, "Make me fall in love with God." That was it. She was gone, and I continued to wash dishes, forgetting about the encounter.

Three months later a January blizzard closed down the city. Everything stopped and became silent and peaceful. The sky had an orange glow. People who would not normally talk to each other did just that. Schools were closed, and we were unable to go to work.

The next day we had to shovel out. My brother shoveled out a parking spot in front. He asked me to stand in the spot while he got his car from the back so that no one would park there. I went down the front steps to cross the street. It was a beautiful day, still and very silent, with few people out and no traffic noises. The sky still had the pretty glow.

As I started to cross the snow-packed road, I noticed a man was walking toward me from my left. He was the most beautiful man I had ever seen. He had a light in his face, and his eyes knew me. I knew he knew me and that he loved me the way that I wanted to be loved. All this went through my mind in seconds. He started coming toward me. I got scared and turned away from him. I saw his face fall as he passed by me. A blanket was slung across his back with something heavy in it, which looked like it could have been a body. I thought that if I went over and opened the blanket, I would see myself in it. But I didn't do that. I got to the other side of the street, turned around, and he was gone. He just vanished.

I stood on the street stunned, trying to understand what had happened. I couldn't tell anyone (and didn't for a long time) because I knew everyone would think I was crazy. But intuitively I knew it was an encounter with Jesus. Also, I knew from that moment that I wanted to know who this was who loved me like this. I started reading the Bible every day, going to Mass every day, etc. I stayed toward the back and tried to get comfortable again. I knew I needed to go to Confession. The Lord, in a miraculous way, helped me run to the springs of His mercy there.

After that, God put lots of things in my path to bring me back. I found all sorts of books "accidentally" that deepened my prayer life and relationship to God. I knew from that time on that I wouldn't get married but that I would find a way to give myself completely to Christ.

Jesus gave me back the vocation I had as a child, and now I have been in religious life thirty-four years. I have a joy in life that I know I would not have had any other way, because I know I am where God wants me. And He is here with me!

Sr. Anne Marie Walsh *is a member of the Society of Our Lady of the Most Holy Trinity, praying and working together for twenty-five years with other SOLT sisters, priests, and laity in the New Evangelization in the modern world, in areas of deepest apostolic need. Her blog is called Musings of a Missionary in the Modern World.*

My Amazing Grace Story in Three Stages

Diane Roe

1. Who was I before?

I WAS THE person in the song, "Amazing Grace." I was lost, and I was blind.

I became lost at an early age through a circumstance that I had no control over, but it set me on the wrong path. I grew up in New York in a family of eight. My mom was Catholic, and my dad was Lutheran. Every Sunday he stayed home while she faithfully took us to church.

When I was eight years old, a drunk driver killed my sixteen-year-old brother, Donald. I remember Donald as the good boy in the family. After his death, I heard everyone say, "Because he was a good boy, he is with God in Heaven." Well, that's how my eight-year-old mind interpreted his death and that's how I got off on the wrong path.

As a young teenager, I thought it would be safer not to be too good. I didn't want to die. Besides I wanted to have fun. "I might die when I'm sixteen," I thought. The Billy Joel song, "Only the Good Die Young," became my song.

When I was eighteen, my brother Paul, who was twenty-seven, died in a car accident. Paul was like me—a bit rebellious, not a saint like Donnie. My eighteen-year-old mind told me there couldn't be a God. Why would he do this to my parents? Or if there was a God, he was one I didn't want to know!

So I figured it must be fate that controls life—the wrong place at the wrong time.

That year, within eight months, my extended family lost an eighteen-year-old, two twenty-seven-year-olds and a thirty-three-year old. I was convinced I was on the right path, so I went to college and enjoyed myself. I really lived it up. I did well, studied hard, and, oh yes, I still went to church. But God was not part of my life. I got married during college and divorced seven years later. I was lost and blind, but I didn't realize it!

I was still lost and still blind when I remarried. It was a dangerous type of "lost," a dangerous type of "blindness." I say that because everything I was doing, almost everyone else was doing, too. It was a secular "lost," a secular "blindness." I justified my actions and decisions by what pleased me.

My choices definitely were not pleasing to God. I was blind to him, and I figured he was blind to me. But I still went to church—most of the time.

I now realize that Jesus, my Shepherd, was searching for me. With the sight I have now, I can see, as if in a rear-view mirror, back into my life. I see almost exactly when he started calling me out of the woods.

But I had to go through the thorns, the darkness, and several storms first.

In June of 1994, I was forced to resign from my job in North Carolina, a job I loved, after working there for twelve years. The thorns of unforgiveness and resentment took hold in my heart. These thorns caused emotional scars that still prick from time to time. My husband also carried thorns of anger and guilt, and so we planned a new future.

The darkness came in September. My dad was diagnosed with liver cancer and had little time to live. My mother suffered from severe depression. In October, as my husband left for Europe on sabbatical, I went to Florida to take care of my dad and mom. At the time, those three months seemed like the worst period of my life. I was close to my dad and I had to watch him die.

The worst part about it was that I had little, if any, faith. I had no idea who God was, or where he was, or if he was. I was lost in darkness! I was angry; I was mad at life. I was with my dad when he died two days after Christmas.

We got back to North Carolina in January and started planning to move from there. Where would we go? I started to get sick—ulcer pains I thought. It made sense after what I have been through, right? I went to the doctor and that night he called me to tell me I was pregnant. I was scared. I was not in control of my life.

A month later, we received a terrific job opportunity in Dallas. I was not happy trading the lush green of North Carolina for the dry brown of Texas. We moved to Dallas in June and six weeks later came my premature daughter. I don't think I adjusted very well to my new life as a mom. I was definitely not in control, and it was not easy. But I still went to church.

2. What God-moment happened to change me?

The storm came.

My husband and I started having serious marital problems. I was stressed, depressed—you name it. Were we headed for divorce?

Jesus found me in the middle of this storm in February of 1998. One night, crying my eyes out in agony, I knelt down and turned to God, if he was there, for help. I acknowledged all my past sins and asked him to do whatever it takes. I said, "Perhaps this marriage was not your plan for me, God? If you want this marriage dissolved, then I will trust you. If you want it to stay intact, please show me the way."

That night I had an awesome experience, which I can't really explain. I felt a big comforting hug engulfing me as I slept. The storm ceased. I awoke to recall that awesome feeling, knowing something had happened.

What was amazing was that I also had a *déjà vu* feeling, a familiar presence that stayed with me.

The day I found my way to a support group, everything just started falling into place. As I look back, it was like a dam bursting open, filled with life jackets.

I learned to "let go and let God." I was smiling again. I had found new friends to share my experiences, friends who cared. I wanted new life; I could feel it. Yes, I was still going to church. I had always gone to church; I was a good Catholic! But now I *wanted* to go to church. I was listening, and I was hearing for the first time. My ears and heart were suddenly open to the things the deacon at our parish was preaching. The pieces began to fall into place; everything made sense—God desired to be in control of my life! Would I let him?

A wonderful woman sat next to me in church one day. She saw the tears in my eyes as I struggled to sing. That angel was the deacon's wife. She held out a hand to me and soon became my spiritual mentor.

3. Who am I now?

By God's grace and mercy working through her and many others, I became a woman on fire for God, reading the Bible and feeling that thirst for the Word, for truth. I have discovered that God is *always* there for us and that *he* will continue to feed us if we are open. I learned that he is always calling us if we will just listen. All the answers are in God's Word and his Church. All the answers are with Jesus!

Once Jesus touches your heart like this, you realize you must respond daily, you must follow him. You don't respond out of duty or guilt. I respond out of pure love, gratitude, and thanksgiving because I was lost and have been found, was blind but now I see.

I know I can see, because my perspective has turned 180 degrees. I once thought divorce, abortion, capital punishment, violent movies, etc. were acceptable. Now I see the exact opposite. I see that God has a plan for each one of us. He allows every situation because every situation, good or bad, brings about the opportunity for sight, for renewal, for rebirth, for transformation, for life—spiritual life through a personal relationship with Jesus!

I was lost, but I have been found; I was blind, but now I see. It is all due to my personal relationship with Jesus.

***Diane Roe** is a wife, mother, and former researcher in biochemical genetics at Baylor University Medical Center in Dallas, TX. A former catechist, she leads the women's Bible study at Our Lady of the Lake Parish in Rockwall, TX, and works with Augustine Institute of Theology, of which she is an alumna.*

Evangelization in the Deep South

Jennifer Fitz

IN 1988, MY barely-Catholic family moved from Metro DC to a small town in South Carolina. My mom had been trying for years to get our family back to Mass, and now she pounced: "Everyone in this town expects you to go to church. We're going to church."

We did. In 1991, I graduated high school with a plaque from the Knights of Columbus declaring me "Catholic Student of the Year." Within weeks of starting college, I quit attending Mass.

College, even in the South, is a great place to lose your faith. By the time I graduated, I was entirely non-Christian and happy with it. My husband Jon and I married in a civil ceremony—I could have gotten a picturesque church wedding at my parent's historic home parish, but it would have been fake. I had too much respect for the Church to claim to be something I wasn't.

But I wasn't really happy. I spent several years trying this and that in the spiritual cafeteria. We attended the local Unitarian Universalist congregation, but it never really took. On a trip to San Antonio, I discovered the depth of my departure from God when I visited one of the historic mission churches, still an active Catholic parish; I entered the church and could not feel the presence of God.

I knew then that I had gone terribly, terribly astray. Something had to change.

Later that year, driving home by myself from a road trip in Virginia, I prayed to God in desperation. I received an immediate response: An inner voice told me to quit doing nothing and to jump in and practice whatever faith was at hand. Buddhism came to mind. Back home, Jon observed: "This is the South. It's Christian. Let's start there."

A friend attending the local Evangelical seminary patiently answered our questions and gave us some pointers. We visited churches and landed in a nondenominational Evangelical congregation that Jon and I both loved instantly. "Nondenominational" felt safe to tell all my liberal friends. It didn't sound churchy. I wasn't ready to go public as a fundamentalist just yet.

I went to Mass on my own a few times a month, and Jon and I settled in as Evangelicals on Sunday mornings. I felt at home and, if you had asked me, I would have said I was a Christian. But I was praying, "Jesus, are you real?"

In the meantime, I began researching the differences between Catholics and Evangelicals. On a Wednesday morning in February 1999, I walked into a colleague's cubicle for our regular monthly business meeting. He was a Baptist deacon in his spare time and we'd talk about religious things. I knew he was praying for me.

"I think I've figured out how to reconcile the Catholic and Protestant views of salvation," I announced. I started to launch into an account of my latest reading, and he stopped me mid-sentence. "Hold on," he said, grabbing his pocket New Testament off his bookshelf. "We need this." He led me to the cafeteria to talk.

We didn't chat about theology—though I read in *Catholic Answers* shortly afterward that I'd pieced together roughly the same vein of thought as the *Joint Declaration on the Doctrine of Justification* and felt vindicated.

Rather, my coworker led me down the Romans Road, straight out of the Evangelical playbook. His Bible was highlighted with all the essential quotes, to make his evangelizing that much more efficient. "Do you accept Christ as your Lord and Savior?" he asked me.

The power of the Holy Spirit was palpable. I knew that this was my moment: I could say "Yes" to Jesus now, or say it never.

We went outside to the picnic tables, and I said the Sinner's Prayer.

And from that moment, I felt Death vanish. Gone. No longer a threat. I was saved.

And as I walked back into the office building, I was filled with an overwhelming desire to get to Mass as soon as I possibly could.

Back at my desk, I flipped through the Yellow Pages. The next Mass in town would be at eight o'clock the next morning. I made plans to arrive late to work. I would have given up my job to be at that Mass. There was no resisting. It was God. He'd answered my prayer. I was in.

What happened to me after I returned to the Catholic faith is that I learned how to think.

Before I became a Christian, I divided the world of ideas into three categories: facts, concepts, and arguments. "Facts" were things like the answers to math problems. "Concepts" were fluid—things that were true because you believed them, not because they were facts. "Arguments" were the machine that chewed up facts and concepts and spit out persuasive opinions.

Several years before my conversion, I had been confronted with the desperate inadequacy of a world without objective truth. It happened in my first-year accounting course. As is common in school, our instructor divided our class into three groups and assigned each group the job of arguing a different position on a question of how to handle an accounting transaction.

I knew, after studying the problem, that the position my group had been assigned was not the best way to represent the financial situation. But I had been trained to argue and argue well, so that's what I did. I came to class and presented the arguments for my group's assigned position. To my horror, my instructor, who had previously held the position I knew to be the correct one, *was persuaded by my arguments into accepting the wrong answer.*

It was sickening.

That incident didn't cause me to pull religion into the realm of truth-or-falsehood, but it did make me painfully aware of how dangerous it is to toy with the truth.

Thus, years later when I returned to the Church, it was first along the path of spiritual exploration, yes, but a path that finally funneled into a single question: Is this true? *Jesus, are you real?*

God is a person (three persons, technically), not a force of nature, and so the proofs for the existence of God are like the proofs for the existence of any other person. My initial moment of conversion was when God opened the door and said, "Come on in." It was an experience, an encounter, not something you can hold out as evidence to others.

No sooner had I re-entered the Church than evidence was demanded of me. My still-Protestant husband had decades of doubts about the Catholic faith, and many well-meaning friends sought to dissuade me from what they viewed as a horrible mistake. I had to learn how to reason: how to identify the truth and how to present it to others.

Arguing ceased to be a tool for swaying opinions and became a tool for discovering and proclaiming what is objectively true. Arguments could be built on logic, on hard evidence (such as historical proof for the existence of the Church), on experience—but always they had to be built on the truth and ordered toward improving our understanding of the truth.

For the first time in my life, I learned how to think straight. All the tools for building arguments that I had acquired at school had been given to me to use however I wanted, for my own ends. Now my mind was finally introduced to the end for which it was created.

Other changes, of course, flowed from that. When you become serious about seeking the truth, you start realizing there are ways you need to change your life. But at the foundation, the first and most potent gift I received with the gift of faith was the gift of reason.

***Jennifer Fitz** is the author of* Classroom Management for Catechists *from Liguori Publications. She is a contributor to many books, websites, and magazines on catechesis and Catholic spirituality, including* The Catholic Mom's Prayer Companion *and* Word by Word: Slowing Down with the Hail Mary. *She blogs for The Catholic Conspiracy and on her personal website, JenniferFitz.com.*

No Perfect Church

Margaret Reveira

IN THE MIDST of an emotional crisis in March 1984, I accepted Jesus Christ as my Savior. I thought I had known him previously, since I attended Mass daily in my parish and was quite involved in a myriad of activities. I eventually realized, though, that all of my labors did not equate to intimacy and, for that reason, it was necessary to pursue a personal relationship with him. It is a decision that I have never regretted.

Almost immediately after I confessed Jesus as Lord, a close friend who was instrumental in my desire to follow him began a non-stop recitation *against* Catholicism. She specified the many reasons why I was to leave the Church and insisted that my blessings from God would be delayed unless I was obedient in this one matter. I understood that I needed to grow in the Word, but I was reluctant to put aside what had been the core of my life since infancy.

I continued to attend Mass, as well as services in various nondenominational churches both in New York

City where I reside and in the surrounding counties. The same friend encouraged me to participate in a small fellowship on Long Island where she and her family were members. To say that I did not fit in is an understatement at best. Anti-Catholicism was prevalent, and it seemed that many individuals there would go out of their way to chat about the perils of the Church. Aside from the obligatory hug exchanged during a particular point in the service, there was minimal camaraderie. Indeed, the "I love you, sister" was not at all expansive, and I realized that I was unable to remain. I remarked to my friend, "You will never understand. I am there by myself, and it is rare that anyone will go out of their way to make me feel welcome. You can talk against Catholicism as much as you want, yet in my parish I am known and greeted by name during Mass and at all times." We maintained our friendship, but, aside from an occasional women's group meeting, I refused to go back.

At the suggestion of an acquaintance, I went to a singles meeting that was affiliated with a church in Rockland County. There I spoke to a man who had been a member of my parish but recently had left to join that same church. There was no disparagement of Catholicism, and I enjoyed myself immensely. Of my own volition, I began to attend their services periodically.

Several issues ultimately caused me to leave the Catholic Church in February 1995. I was restless, I was bored, and I knew that I was in need of a change, as well as a manifestation of God's Word in my life. For a while, I stayed home on Sundays. Then, with teaching tapes and my Bible in hand, I returned to the same church in Rockland County, followed by one in New Jersey. I enjoyed the services in both places, but why did I feel that something was missing?

In May 1998, I became a member of a megachurch in New York City. I met my husband there exactly one year later, and we married in November 2001. Both of us were on the volunteer staff and very involved, yet I felt a distinct uneasiness. I had often heard that there was no spiritual accountability in Catholicism and that people were essentially free to do as they pleased. In this particular atmosphere, I observed how many of the congregants, several of whom were fellow volunteers, lived in direct contradiction to God's Word. When I began to question or challenge them in conversation, their responses were, "God doesn't judge me—he knows I'm a work in progress, and he'll bless me by the sincerity of my heart." I was unable to fathom how this was allowed to occur within a purportedly Christian environment. The atrocities flourished.

With the influx of celebrities and speakers who seemed to advocate things that contradicted the Bible, the church sanctuary gradually became devoid of the Lord's presence. I also witnessed how many of the attendees freely worshiped the pastor but knew little about the Risen Savior. During that period, I began to long for holiness, order, and adherence to the Word of God, all of which are basic principles of our faith. Isaiah 5:20 states: "Woe to those who call evil good and good evil, who put darkness for light and light for darkness, who put bitter for sweet and sweet for bitter." During that time, I found myself not only having to defend the Faith, but telling others that the majority of Catholics whom I had known were sincere godly people who would prefer to die rather live a sordid lifestyle.

When my husband and I resigned from this megachurch in June 2008, the Lord began to urge me to return to the Catholic Church. Rather than obey immediately, I shared the revelation with friends. Based on their responses, I assumed that I had not heard his voice. But the Lord is so gracious, for he continued to speak to my spirit until finally, in mid-2011, I could no longer deny his will for my life. My husband, who is not Catholic, supported this decision. In September of that year, I joined my local parish, Our Lady of Grace and, in essence, returned home, resuming my previous level of involvement there and, after that parish was closed in 2015, at my current parish, St. Frances of Rome. I continue to accompany my husband to a non-denominational fellowship in our neighborhood, but I am proudly and boldly Catholic. The Lord has placed a fervency within my heart, and it is a joy to share the tenets of my faith with others.

I remember speaking with a man back in 1990 whom I had met at the singles fellowship five years earlier. By this point, he had returned to the Catholic faith. When I asked what prompted his decision, he replied, "There is no perfect church, but there is a perfect God." Nearly thirty years later, his answer has continued to resonate within me.

Margaret Reveira *is a lifelong New Yorker who has worked in law enforcement for the last thirty-eight years. She and her husband reside in Bronx County where she joyfully participates in her parish, St. Frances of Rome.*

From New Age to Eyes of Faith

Lyn Mettler

HOW I "CAME AROUND" to Catholicism truly shocks me utterly to the core. It's not that it was some huge, dramatic moment, but the simple fact of me becoming Catholic is nothing I could ever have imagined. If anyone had told me it would happen, I would have denied it vehemently.

Although exposed to different Protestant churches growing up, I always felt most comfortable in a spiritual but non-religious environment. I was baptized in the Southern Baptist Church, attended a Disciples of Christ Church in high school and attended Methodist and Presbyterian churches with friends in college. None of it stuck. After college, I spent many years studying various New Age philosophies. I always believed in God, but not in religion as a requirement to get to God. However, through all that, I never felt that I was given a solid, specific path to self-improvement, which was something I had always been seeking—a way to become a better version of myself. All I found in New Age philosophies was wishy-washy. Try this. Do that. It was so disorganized; I never got very far.

Catholicism, once I began to investigate it, offered me a structured path to self-improvement, something that had worked for countless others before me, helping them reach a higher calling and, ultimately become the people God designed them to be—saints. Regular Confession helps bring to mind those issues that need improvement, weekly Mass brings you into communion with God, set times of prayer help you begin to incorporate quiet, reflective times into your day. But, of course, Catholicism is so much more than a routine to help with self-improvement, as I would soon learn.

Right around Christmas of 2011, I experienced my "calling." I don't even know what words to give this. I've heard "calling" and "conversion of heart" but to me, it's like suddenly I was given the eyes of faith, as if a light switch was flipped from "off" to "on." Never before was I willing to believe in Jesus as the Son of God, because my very logical mind would not accept it. But once I had the eyes of faith, it didn't need to be proven to me. Suddenly, I could just feel how right it was.

A few years before that I had begun to feel a faint desire and interest in revisiting the place where my husband and I spent our Catholic marriage retreat. Feeling "pulled" or "drawn" to that site is the best way I can describe it. It was deep in the recesses of my mind, or perhaps I was feeling the stirrings of the Holy Spirit.

I looked up the retreat center on the web and learned more about it, but then I ignored this stirring for a couple of years. Eventually I went back to the retreat center and spent a silent retreat, which led me to my blog. All of a sudden, just before Christmas 2011, I began to feel more strongly that I'd like to go to Catholic Mass. So I gathered the whole family—my husband, and two young boys—and off we went.

My husband is a cradle Catholic, although he had not been engaged with the Church since he left his parents' home. I had never been interested in Catholicism and was turned off by it. Although I had attended Mass many times when visiting his parents, themselves devout Catholics and models of the faith, I had always felt very uncomfortable. Everyone knelt and said things and made the Sign of the Cross, none of which I understood and all of which made me feel left out and unsure of myself. So, every time I went, I would sit without kneeling or saying anything or genuflecting, all the while feeling pretty left out and embarrassed. Just walking into a Catholic church made me feel quite uncomfortable.

Our marriage retreat was probably the first time I can remember feeling good in a Catholic setting. I remember the peaceful feeling of being away from the noise of the outside world—no TVs, no radios, only the two of us. And I finally saw the beauty of the Mass when we attended as a couple together, just us, in this quiet setting.

But at that Mass to which I was inexplicably drawn seventeen years after our marriage retreat, didn't seem as bad as I had remembered. In fact, if I dared admit it, it felt kind of good. We went back again to the same church for Christmas Eve Mass. I decided to give it my full effort, ignoring those feelings of inadequacy and embarrassment for the sake of my boys, kneeling, singing, and reading the responses. Just like our marriage retreat, it was the complete and utter peace that stood out to me, something that was lacking in my life as the mother of two young boys and owner of a small business.

This simple respite of peace once a week was delightful. The positive feelings grew from there into a great "thirst" and unquenchable desire to learn everything I could and attend Mass as often as possible. Then into complete and utter joy, even moments of ecstasy, I would daresay now.

Perhaps this happened at Christmas because that is when we celebrate Christ's coming into the world. I feel the Holy Spirit allowed Christ to be born in me at this time. Why this Christmas and not seventeen Christmases earlier? Everything happens in God's time, and he knows when our hearts are best prepared to receive him. My grandmother, not a Catholic but a strong Christian and a faithful woman, had recently passed, and I feel in my heart that she must have been praying for me in Heaven. She was always very concerned about my lack of belief in Jesus Christ.

Since Christmas Eve Mass in 2011, I have rarely missed Mass. And it's less because I'm obligated to go than because I can't stand to miss. I joined the Church at Easter 2013 and was ecstatic to finally be a part of the Body of Christ, the Church, and to strive to grow into the saint God intends me to be. After many long months of desiring the Eucharist, I was finally able to receive Communion, to join Church life in all its fullness, and to help others along their journey.

I have discerned that, for now, God is asking me to help others through their questions, misunderstandings, and misgivings about Catholicism. I try to help them through my blog, as well as being actively involved in our parish's RCIA program for new Catholics. I teach religious education to help instill a love for, and a personal relationship with, Jesus Christ in our youth and I proclaim God's Word as a reader at daily and Sunday Mass.

To me, this is utterly a miracle. I can explain it no other way. I still stop and ask, "Is this me?" and begin to doubt myself a bit, but then I remember how it feels to offer myself up fully to our Lord, and I "get it" again and again and again.

To anyone considering the Catholic faith, I pray that you experience a conversion of heart as I did and that God gives you eyes of faith. I am not sure why God called me and suddenly gave me this gift. That is not for me to know. Open your heart. Participate in Mass (kneel and make the sign of the Cross even if you're unsure). Study the Catholic faith. Pray unceasingly. Ask many questions and see where it leads you. I hope it leads you to the place of peace that I have found.

Lyn Mettler *was a nonbeliever for more than thirty years. She never dreamed she'd be Catholic and passionately so. A wife and mother living in Zionsville, IN, Lyn has worked in journalism and public relations and runs a public relations and travel writing business, blogging* at *A Catholic Newbie and Go To Travel Gal.*

Answering the Call by Taking the Leap!

Virginia Lieto

CONVERSION EXPERIENCES can come upon you gradually, or all at once. In my case, it was extremely gradual, more of a series of conversions, with one building upon another over my lifetime. I am a "cradle" Catholic, having attended both Catholic grade school and high school. Growing up, I dutifully received the Sacraments. In my twenties and into my early thirties, I would categorize myself as a lukewarm Catholic: running through the motions of doing what was expected, attending Mass on Sundays.

In my late thirties, during an employment layoff as a result of a bank merger, I began placing my trust in Jesus. During my layoff, I traveled from New Jersey to Utah to become godmother to my friend's baby. While in the Salt Lake City area, I looked around and noticed how beautiful the area was, how friendly the people were, and took a leap of faith—I got a job in Utah!

We had four wonderful years in Utah. Since Utah is predominantly Mormon, many of my Mormon friends asked me questions about the Catholic faith. In answering those questions, I realized how much I needed to learn about my faith in order to explain it adequately to others. This is where God planted the seed for what would become my life's work. During this time in my life, I believe God called me to serve him. Yet I felt unqualified, as I did not have all of the answers to all of the questions asked of me. So, I put God on hold and did not answer the call at this time.

After four years in Utah, and because of another bank merger, we moved to Charlotte, North Carolina. My husband's faith and mine had grown stronger while in Utah, to the extent that we based our housing decision on proximity to a Catholic church where the Holy Spirit was busy at work. We found Saint Thomas Aquinas Catholic Church, served by Franciscan Friars. The minute I walked into the church, I knew I was "home," because of the warmth and welcome given by the Franciscans. Although I still felt unqualified in knowledge of the faith, God really put me to work in this parish. I got involved with parish activity, participating on the Finance Council, chairing the Evangelization and Communication Commission, the Evangelization Ministry, and a Capital Campaign!

All the while, though, volunteer work wasn't enough. I wanted more—to learn more. I wanted to be able to connect the dots for those inquiring about the Catholic faith and to serve God better. The burning desire to change my life was building dramatically. I worked as a technology audit manager, which was getting tiresome. God was speaking to me, and I decided to finally answer the call and take another leap of faith.

In 2011, I retired from the bank auditing profession. At the same time, I committed my life to God. On the eve of enrolling in school to obtain my Master of Arts in Pastoral Theology, I stood in the bedroom with my husband and asked him, "Do you think I'm doing the right thing?"

He responded in a rather official voice, "The Lord finds favor with your plan."

We both looked at each other as if we didn't know where those words or sound of the voice came from, and we both knew, instantly, that it was the Holy Spirit speaking. We didn't need any more confirmation. We both knew that I *must* do this. Not knowing where this would all lead, I took the leap of faith.

I believe that God's plan for me is far better than anything which I could conceive. With that commitment and my faith, I obtained a Master of Arts Degree in Pastoral Theology from Saint Joseph's College of Maine in 2014. In my studies, I learned a great deal about Church history, Biblical studies, moral values, and Catholic social teaching. Specifically, during my studies, I realized that the way for me to connect the dots for others was through the virtues, for Jesus is the Way. My "call within a call" is to focus on the virtues, evangelizing both adults, through my public speaking, and children through my picture books. By embracing the virtues, we can grow closer to God and live happier lives. My life's focus now is to bring the virtues to the forefront of our lives and share them with others.

With degree in hand, I can truly attest that the commitment to give my life to God has been the best decision of my life. God's plan for me has brought me so much joy.

God qualified me, the unqualified, to give me what I need to do His will. He has given me so much knowledge and confidence! God keeps me extremely busy, yet He is the best boss ever.

Virginia Lieto, *author, speaker, and theology professor, earned an MA in Pastoral Theology from Saint Joseph's College of Maine, where she is an adjunct professor for the online Theology program. She writes the award-winning children's book series,* Adventures of Faith, Hope and Charity *and contributes to* Catechist Magazine, *Catholic Mom, Saint Joseph's College of Maine's theology blog, and her personal blog at VirginiaLieto.com.*

The Annoying Lesson of Humanae Vitae

Brian Gill

MY PARENTS WERE part of a nice, normal, mainstream Protestant church. I accepted what I was taught there and still do to a great extent. But I never stopped learning more about what I believed. That eventually made me realize that what I had seen as Christian faith was a small piece of a much larger reality.

I was a Christian when the 1960s began, which wasn't unusual for Americans living in the upper Midwest. The exciting, or disturbing, decade ended when I was eighteen. I still thought of myself as Christian in 1970, which may be a bit remarkable.

What passed for Christian radio in my area featured nice music, passionate preachers, and a virulently anti-Catholic attitude. Their version of "fire and brimstone" faith focused on guilt and damnation, with the occasional gleeful exultation over roasting sinners. That's what my memory tells me, at any rate. I don't have any recordings or transcripts of what they said—only the memories of an early teen. I was going through the early stages of depression, which may have affected my perceptions. What I have learned from others, though, suggests that my memories aren't very far from the mark.

Venom-spitting radio Christians, along with all that was happening in America and the world, started me wondering if religion was a psychiatric disorder. But folks like my parents, who were Christian but not crazy, helped me realize that lunatics can be frightfully religious but that religion wasn't necessarily lunacy.

Christian radio's unrelenting message of doom and hopelessness helped me learn to love rock and roll—on a different station. (I've since learned that much of the upper Midwest wasn't nearly as anti-Catholic as where I grew up and neither was Christian radio.)

Lurid radio rants against the Catholic Church's manifold transgressions got me curious: how could an organization so corrupt, so wicked, be allowed to exist in a civilized society? More to the point, why couldn't I see any evidence of all those evil deeds?

Things and people that should make sense, but don't, bother me—a lot. Without my being particularly aware of it, my mind started an "in-basket" for facts about the Catholic Church—facts, not assertions. I knew the difference before leaving my teens.

I'm a very emotional man, and I've learned that my emotions make very poor counselors. Refusing to trust my feelings helped me survive my first suicidal impulse, in my mid-teens. I realized that what I was feeling, awful as it was, probably wouldn't outlast me. Being an extremely stubborn person, I thought I could out-endure the pain. As it turns out, I was right. I've learned more about why suicide is a bad idea, and how prayer can help—a lot. Knowing that I've got spiritual backup is good.

A system of belief that's mostly an emotional rush wouldn't appeal to me. As soon as the excitement ebbed, I'd start wondering why I'd been so revved up—and whether I should be concerned about what had gotten past my defenses. Something that I could still believe when I felt like all the color and beauty was drained from the world—that, I'd pay attention to. And take much more seriously.

I've had very positive experiences with non-ranting Protestants, and even "felt saved"—for maybe ten or fifteen minutes. Maybe a little longer. Oddly enough, I've never experienced that as a Catholic, which, for someone like me is probably just as well.

A huge turning point came just before my wife and I got married. I knew that I'd have to agree that our children, if any, would be raised in the Catholic faith. This meant that, just to learn what I was agreeing to, I had to start a sort of crash course of study. Close to the top of my "worrisome" list was the Church's stand on artificial contraceptives. I really, really didn't want the Catholic Church to be right about that.

The key document for the issue was *Humanae Vitae.* I got the official English translation and studied it. I'm fairly sharp, and my experience with other Christian denominations suggested that I'd find gaps in the Vatican's logic I could drive a truck through. But I failed. I didn't find a gap in the document's reasoning. So I went through it again. Second time, same result.

At this point, I felt very frustrated. I could reject the conclusions of *Humanae Vitae,* but to do so I'd have to reject ideas such as God being real and having created the world. I was not willing to do that, hormonally-addled or not. That experience taught me a respect for the Catholic Church that no other outfit had earned.

Years later, I grudgingly admitted to myself that I had learned who currently held the authority that our Lord gave Peter. That's in Matthew 16:13–19, after Simon Peter says, "You are the Christ, the Son of the living God."

At that point, I could have decided that I would rather walk away from our Lord than become a Catholic. Or I could formally sign up with the Church and keep following Jesus, which seemed like a much more reasonable choice. I hadn't wanted to become a Catholic. When what I learned forced the decision, I was annoyed as much as anything.

But there were and are aspects of the Church I enjoy. For one thing, the Catholic Church really is "catholic," universal. We're not tied to one country, or one culture, or one ethnic group. Catholics are certainly not people who get together because we all like the same things. We all are, or should be, following Jesus and sharing the Good News with anyone who will listen. And that's another topic.

Brian Gill *lives in Minnesota and has four children, a background in history, a checkered work history, and a guardedly hopeful attitude toward human goofiness that gives him a different perspective. He is interested in what exists in the universe, what exists beyond, and what might exist.*

Swept into the Heart of the Church

Melanie Jean Juneau

MY PARENTS RAISED me in a cool, calm, and conservative Presbyterian church where *nobody* talked about a personal relationship with Jesus, and no one talked about accepting Christ's forgiveness, allowing Jesus to save us, or committing our lives to God. However, as a Protestant child who went to Sunday School from age three into my mid-teens, I grew up on the stories of Jesus, singing songs about his love, and memorizing Bible verses.

I was a prayerful kid; I sensed God was close to me even as a small child. One of my Sunday School teachers, who I realize now was close to God, always turned to me to interpret passages of Scripture in class, then beamed at my responses afterward. After I had committed my life to God at age sixteen, my mum recalled that this teacher repeatedly told her, "You know, Melanie is a child of God."

Intimacy with God

Listening to an Evangelical friend in high school stirred a yearning in me for deeper intimacy with God, but I did not know how to go about it. When I was sixteen, teenagers were invited for the first time to the National Conference of Canadian Presbyterian ministers, missionaries, and elders. My frustrated desire to learn how to connect with God in a real way drove me to stand up in front of all those leaders in our church and challenge them: "After eleven years of faithful Sunday School attendance, why did no one tell me it was even possible to have a personal relationship with Jesus? Do I have to go to the Jesus People or the Pentecostals to learn how to be filled with the Holy Spirit?"

Of course, everyone clapped as I sat down with my heart pounding. A lovely missionary, with her silver hair swept up in an elegant bun and her eyes twinkling with the love of God, asked me,

"Have you accepted Jesus as your Savior?"

I was baffled, "I am not sure; I don't think so."

She looked at me, really looked into my eyes, "I am sure you already have, because just now you spoke in the Spirit, with his power and clarity. Just to make sure, when you are in your room tonight, ask Jesus to forgive your sins and accept the salvation he offers you. Then commit your life to Christ. Tomorrow we will pray together for the infilling of his Holy Spirit."

That night, I felt foolish, like I was speaking to thin air, but I said the words, committing my life to Christ. I was immediately filled with joy, experiencing a tangible sense of love for the first time. It felt like a warm blanket was enveloping me.

Monday at school, all the Evangelicals and Jesus people gathered around, hugging me. "Your face is shining! You did it—you accepted Christ, didn't you?"

Of course, these kids talked me into attending their weekly Friday night Jesus Party. My sister and I nervously took the bus from my perfectly groomed suburb to a church in the center of town. I was terrified as I walked down the stairs into a huge basement hall with hundreds of young people dancing, shaking tambourines, and singing in tongues. Thankfully, my desire for more of God was stronger than my fear.

Later, as I stood in a baptismal pool up to my waist, I was still so uptight I only managed to squeak out a few words in tongues as the pastor laid hands on me, praying for the Baptism of the Holy Spirit. It was not until later that night, in the solitude of my room, that the gift of tongues was released, filling me once again with a sense of freedom and joy for my growing life in God.

For the next year, I was in the midst of the "honeymoon stage" with God which lead me once again out of my comfort zone and into a church I would never have chosen on my own.

This IS the Body of Christ

The next year I moved to another city to attend university. I was shocked to discover that the only place alive in the Spirit was a Catholic charismatic prayer group. I was confused—how could Catholics be filled with the Holy Spirit? I assumed God merely tolerated these Catholics' heretical faith. I was sure God would soon show them the truth, that they only needed faith in Jesus and the Bible. Period.

By mid-semester, I decided to accompany fellow students from the prayer meeting to a University Mass. I was so shocked and overwhelmed by the powerful presence of God in that small University Chapel, I could barely follow the rest of the young people as they stood, kneeled, and sat. When I heard the priest say, "Behold, the Lamb of God, who takes away the sin of the world" and "Happy are those who are called to his supper," I suddenly wanted—no I *craved*—the Eucharist. Of course, my Catholic friends told me I could not receive Holy Communion that evening but suggested I make an appointment with one of the Jesuits the next day.

The next day, the Jesuit chaplain asked me, "Why do you want to become a Catholic?"

My answer was simple: "Well, if the Eucharist really is the Body of Christ, I want to receive it. Is that selfish?"

The priest beamed at me.

It was embarrassing but every time I attended Mass while I was going through instruction to become Catholic, tears streamed down my face because I could not receive the Eucharist yet. The tears were not the result of anything I could verbalize but were rooted in an inexpressible longing placed deep in my spirit by God.

Caught by Mary

A couple of months later, I was living with a Catholic charismatic family. I could not sleep for a few nights. After I stumbled out of my bedroom one night, desperate for relief, they prayed with me and discerned that the reason I could not sleep was that God had been shining his light into my heart, preparing a room for Mary. Would I invite Mary into my heart?

Sitting right there, exhausted from lack of sleep, and despite all the Protestant theological objections in my head, I surrendered to God's inner promptings and said yes to Mary. Joy and peace flooded my soul instantly.

Well, when Mary lives in your heart and God places a hunger for the Eucharist in your heart, nobody wants you *but* the Catholic Church. Within six months, I joined the Church, much to my family's despair, receiving three Sacraments in two days. My grandfather lamented over my conversion: "My God, how did she get herself into that mess?"

Caught and Taught

Pope Francis explains that a relationship with Christ is not just for Protestant Evangelicals but for Catholics, who are then safeguarded by the Roman Catholic Church. An authentic Christian cannot be a "free agent":

> On the contrary, you cannot love God without loving your brothers, you cannot love God outside of the Church; you cannot be in communion with God without being so in the Church, and we cannot be good Christians if we are not together with those who seek to follow the Lord Jesus, as one single people, one single body, and this is the Church. (Pope Francis, General Audience, June 25, 2014)

I was converted through God's direct intervention, as well as by believers who lived in Christ as he lived in them. These faithful Christians prepared my heart to listen to the words of a knowledgeable Jesuit priest who answered all my questions and doubts with wisdom.

My spiritual experiences occurred in the family of God. I was caught by God, then taught by brothers and sisters, and swept right into the heart of his Church.

***Melanie Jean Juneau** is a Canadian mother of nine children who blogs at Joy of Nine9. Melanie is Editor in Chief of Catholic Stand, as well as being a columnist at Catholic Lane, Catholic Stand, Catholic 365, and CAPC. She is the author of* Echoes of the Divine *and* Oopsy Daisy, *and coauthor of* Love Rebel: Reclaiming Motherhood.

No Turning Back

Kevin Luksus

FROM MY EARLIEST memories, I recall going to Sunday Mass. Mom and Dad raised me in the Catholic faith and sent me to Catholic schools. Catholic practices were a routine part of my life. Outside of church and school, however, I didn't think about God much.

Life had its ups and downs. Schoolwork and baseball were positives. My home life was a negative. I didn't know it at the time, but my mom likely was depressed during most of my childhood. My dad had financial problems with his business, where he worked long hours. By the time I was a teenager, I felt disconnected from my parents.

Throughout high school, I continued to do well academically but had almost no social life. For much of my high school experience, I was miserable, lonely, and felt worthless. During one dark time in my junior year, I thought about suicide. But something happened that night. I couldn't explain why, but I suddenly felt hopeful. I knew I didn't want to give up, that somehow there was something more. I am sure that was the Holy Spirit. From that point on, I was a bit more optimistic, although I didn't have any reason for it. I felt like I was in a hole, I wanted to get out; I just didn't know how.

Surprise Beginning

My journey toward God started surprisingly, and it didn't have anything to do with church. At the end of my junior year in high school, I went to a one-month summer program at an engineering college. The program gave students experience working on cool science projects. I signed up to build a laser communication system, along with another student from southern Indiana. I began to hang around with him and two other guys. The group accepted me readily. Their good sense of humor provided lots of joking around. We did have some serious conversations, though. That month I discovered what it was like to have people accept me for who I am. They even liked me. Those friendships helped me loosen up and develop a sense of humor.

The day we said goodbye, I cried most of the way back home. Something had changed in me. I knew there was more to life—something healthy and good—and I wanted more of it. Although I wouldn't have put it in these words at the time, I wanted more than just to exist. I wanted to *live*.

I tried new things, sometimes acting crazy or goofy. I wasn't trying to make people laugh. I was letting go and being different. But no matter what I did, the happiness I felt at the time was short-lived.

Hunger for God

Sr. Joan Marie, who taught the first semester of my senior religion class, was a little firecracker. Her great sense of humor helped her connect well with students. I remember going through Fr. John Powell's book, *A Reason to Live, a Reason to Die*, and developing a hunger for God.

My high school had evening class retreats twice a year, but I had never paid any attention to them before now. A poor experience on an eighth-grade retreat left me thinking these were a waste of time. But Sr. Joan Marie asked my class to go on the senior fall retreat and, with my newfound openness, I was ready to give it a try. During the sessions, I heard other kids talk about God in their lives. We read and discussed the Scripture in a way I had never done before. The Gospel passages came alive for me.

During Reconciliation at the end of the retreat, I remember thinking, "If God is really there, then it makes sense to live one hundred percent for him. But if he isn't, I might as well just live for myself." I wanted my life to be different, but I was afraid. The enormity of the commitment and the changes it would mean for me were just too much.

Search Retreat Brings Freedom

As January came around, I heard about a weekend retreat called Search. That name fit me because I was searching. This time I was ready for something more. Of the many remarkable experiences that weekend, three in particular were very special.

The first came on Saturday afternoon during our free time. I went to the chapel to talk to God alone. Sitting there, I began to see that God was real. I knew that he was present with me at that moment and that he loved me very much. No matter what happened in the rest of my life, he would be there. It was the most powerful moment of my life. Then and there I decided to let go and give my heart and life to Jesus. I immediately felt at peace, but the full impact of that event was yet to come.

Later, that night at Reconciliation, Fr. Jim Kelly took a long time with each student. When it finally came to me, the depth of all my struggle, alienation, and sin poured out. When I received absolution, I knew I was free. *I was free!*

I should have been tired the next day from lack of sleep, but I felt alive—and yet apprehensive. My decision meant a lot of changes were coming. I wasn't sure if I could go through with it, especially the part about talking to my parents about what happened to me on the retreat. The leaders taped a large sheet of newsprint to the wall, and we drew a symbol of what the retreat meant to us. I made a rising sun. I felt that I had a new start in life and from that point on I have considered it a symbol of my new life in Christ.

When I got home, I tried to talk to my parents. That didn't go well. They didn't understand what I was trying to say, and Mom thought I was telling them I didn't like the way they had raised me. While that was a disappointment, I was still encouraged because I did something I had thought I could never do. From that point on, I prayed and read Scripture for an hour every night. I just gobbled up God's Word. It spoke such words of life and made so much sense in how to live—to really live.

I went to retreat follow-up meetings every other week. For the next six weeks, I experienced a tremendous peace that I had never known—like someone who had been lost for years and finally found his way home. When I faced challenging situations, I would do what I thought God wanted, no matter how painful or embarrassing it was for me, because I had decided there was no going back.

Summer arrived, and the retreat meetings ended suddenly. But I wasn't ready to quit. I still had such a thirst for God. I began to go to an evening prayer meeting at my high school. Most of the time, I was the only student. Through those gatherings, I experienced a different and yet moving way of praying with others. One of the adults told me about a charismatic prayer meeting at a Catholic church in a nearby town. That was a different, but powerful, experience. I occasionally still got together with Fr. Kelly. His listening and advice were incredibly helpful.

I left for college at the end of the summer, not knowing anyone in my college or new city. One of the nuns in the prayer group had given me the name and address of a contact for a prayer group. I was determined not to give up.

The first day at college was busy with placement exams, but on the afternoon of the second day, I rode my bike across town to meet my prayer group contact. When I returned, I met Bill. He had his door open, and I just decided to walk in and say "hello." When he heard where I went, he invited me to join him for a progressive dinner with the Union of Baptist Students. Why not? I went, had a good time, and made some new friends. Arriving back at school, we saw a notice from someone offering to give a ride to midnight Mass at the Catholic Student Center in town. It was my turn to invite Bill.

I discovered the celebrant was the contact for the prayer group. After Mass, Bill and I met Mary, who was hanging out in the lounge. Our motivation for talking to her wasn't spiritual, but God used that meeting to reach my new friend, Mary. One week later she went with us to the prayer meeting. The prayer group was full of people who loved God. Their worship was full of joy.

In my sophomore year, their core group invited me to join them as a student liaison. The leaders were mature disciples, and they helped me grow. Once I struggled with a situation but told no one. A godly woman spoke a word from the Lord that I knew was for me. I knew what to do. The chain of events that followed changed my life, and God once again demonstrated his love and power.

Principles of Conversion

All of this took place forty years ago, and my story continues. Reflecting on my experiences reveals several principles of conversion. First, God is the initiator, but we need to respond. Most of the time I didn't know what I was doing, but that wasn't important. I was doing what God set before me at the time.

Second, his Spirit aroused a hunger within me. God uses the events of life to get our attention; sometimes he speaks in a quiet voice. We should never ignore these movements or let something else take their place. Keep seeking the Lord where he may be found.

Third, when presented with opportunities to surrender to God—let go! I believe the mindset where I told myself, "I'm not turning back," kept me making the hard choices that allowed God to work in my life.

Kevin Luksus, *a Catholic parish leader, family physician, and author, has 37 years of experience in adult faith formation, youth ministry, and men's ministry, as well as creating guide materials for small groups. His passion for the Catholic parish to reach its potential has led an innovative approach to parish transformation, which he shares through his website, Parish Dynamics.*

About Nancy Ward

Nancy H.C. Ward, convert, journalist, author, and speaker, writes from Texas about Catholicism, conversion, and Christian community at NancyHCWard.com, JOYAlive.net, CatholicMom.com, and other websites and magazines. Through her *Sharing Your Catholic Faith Story* workshops and DVD, she shares her conversion story at Catholic parishes and conferences, equipping others to share their own stories. Facilitator of two Catholic Writers Guild critique groups, she also serves on the Guild's Board and speaks at national writers' conferences. Nancy is proud to have contributed to the award-winning *The Catholic Mom's Prayer Companion.*

Nancy's books and DVDs are available from NancyHCWard.com, JOYAlive.net, Amazon.com, and Catholic bookstores.

67689608R00157

Made in the USA
Columbia, SC
30 July 2019